John Brayshaw Kaye

Vashti

A Poem In Seven Books

John Brayshaw Kaye

Vashti
A Poem In Seven Books

ISBN/EAN: 9783744651790

Printed in Europe, USA, Canada, Australia, Japan

Cover: Foto ©Thomas Meinert / pixelio.de

More available books at **www.hansebooks.com**

VASHTI

A POEM IN SEVEN BOOKS

BY

JOHN BRAYSHAW KAYE

Author of
"Songs of Lake Geneva"

G. P. PUTNAM'S SONS

NEW YORK   LONDON
27 WEST TWENTY-THIRD ST.   24 BEDFORD ST., STRAND
The Knickerbocker Press
1894

Electrotyped, Printed and Bound by
The Knickerbocker Press, New York
G. P. Putnam's Sons

PREFACE.

A CONSIDERABLE portion of the following poem, it will be observed, is an adoption of parts of the Bible story of the Book of Esther, with such changes in the language as to make it conform to the measure of the verse chosen ; while a part of the remainder is made up of speech put into the mouths of some of its personages, who in the Bible story are silent, or have but little to say. By this means, and the introduction of a few minor characters, the author has endeavored to bring into more critical prominence the chief characters in the tremendous drama ; ascribing to them motives—and giving their reasoning thereon—which, it is assumed, impelled them to action ; and especially has he sought to give a voice to, and get a hearing for, one of the chief unfortunates in the story—and at the same time one of the most interesting characters of Holy Writ,—that she may relate her trials and sufferings through one of the most singular and pathetic ordeals known to human

experience ; whatever the facts after her deposition may
have been. Around and through this nucleus, the author has attempted to weave and blend what it seems to
him must have been some of the principal events of con-
temporaneous profane history, leading up to, running
through, and continuing a time after the happening of,
the central events recorded in the Book of Esther, and
having a more or less direct effect upon some of its personages and their actions. At the same time the author
has attempted to invest the poem with some hint of the
combined spiritual atmosphere of Judaism and Zoroas-
tianism, the one or the other of which must have influ-
enced its actors to a greater or less extent. In the journey
to Lydia, a journey not recorded in the Book of Esther,
the author has endeavored to have called up some of
the interesting history and legend of the countries
through which the travellers passed, for the edification
of the beautiful and melancholy refugee, and, let him
hope, without the protest of the reader.

But few notes of reference have been made, but then,
in a poem, it can scarcely be required to cite authorities,
still the history of the poem, it is believed, is in the main
correct. With a deep consciousness, however, of its
many imperfections, in expression, arrangement, and
otherwise, the poem *Vashti* is offered to the reading
public in the hope that it may not prove an altogether

unappreciated effort to further exemplify the persistent strength of purpose, and love of race, of Mordecai ; the vigor of mind, the exalted courage and faith of Esther ; and more than all, the kindly, loving, yet strong nature of the fair woman, who, at such peril and sacrifice in the cause of womanly modesty dared to ignore the command of the cruel and imperious Ahasuerus.

JOHN B. KAYE.

CALMAR, I'A., April, 1894.

CONTENTS.

BOOK I.

THE GREAT FAIR AT SHUSHAN.

BOOK IV.

HAMAN'S DECREE—THE MOURNING.

BOOK V.

LITTLE META.

BOOK VI.

ESTHER.

BOOK VII.

THE FLIGHT.

VASHTI.

BOOK I.

OLD Nile had flowed seven times five hundred years
    In his accustomed course, sweeping adown
Those brown Egyptian vistas to the sea,
And had been feared and worshipped as a god
By untold millions who had lived their lives,
And sung their songs, and boasted their exploits
In arms and arts, and then lain down and died ;
Till on his sunny banks on either side—
From the broad Delta unto that far land
Where once the beauteous Queen of Sheba reigned,[1]—
Wrapped in their sere-cloth folds and put away,
A hundred generations lay entombed ;

---

[1] Abyssinia.

The pyramids already were grown old,
And even more of mystery than now
Dwelt on the stony face, so calm and cold,
Of Gizeh's Sphynx.   The Memnon's harp-like voice
A thousand years with each returning sun
Had murmured sweetly from the Theban gates ;
A thousand years had passed since Israel
Toiling across the weary wilderness
'Scaped Pharaoh and bondage ; Canaan's land,
The promised country, had been occupied ;
The world's mutations, and the sweep of years
Had brought to Israel triumphs and deep woes ;
Philistia had been won, and lost again,
Won, lost, and won, and the Twelve Tribes, by turns,
Had warred among themselves, been reconciled,
Been strong, and weak, by times masters, and slaves ;
(And ten had disappeared—who shall say where ?)
Assyria had thundered at the gates
Of David's city ; been repulsed of God,
And lost the sway of empire ; Babylon,
From her encircling walls, to victory
And to Jerusalem, had sent her hosts,
Had razed the Holy City to the ground,
Destroyed its temples, and the house of God,
And brought back Israel to captivity
To last until the captives had beheld

The oppressor's own destruction ; Persian, o'er Mede,
And o'er Chaldean, had prevailed, and o'er
A hundred Asiatic kings and chiefs ;
Had humbled Egypt, brought fierce Libya down,
And levied tribute on the western tribes
To Ethiopia's border ; Macedon and Thrace,
Upon the northern coast of Ægean,
And many islands of the Ægean Sea,
Had bowed their necks unto the Persian yoke ;
E'en the swart warriors 'yond the Ister's¹ course—
The predatory " Scyths beyond the sea,"
Trembled anon in dread expectancy
Lest once again from 'cross the Bosphorus
The Persians and their levies might appear,
In countless numbers, panoplied for war,
And all athirst for plunder, to draw sword
And level lance against the Scythian shafts ;
When from his central throne the mighty King
Ahasuerus—" King of Kings " so called
(Being the same called " Xerxes " by the Greeks)—
Proclaimed a feast and time of merriment,
And military pageant of the realm,
Throughout the provinces sixscore and seven
That filled the limits of his mighty empire,
And bade the kings, and princes, and chief men

¹ Ister, ancient name of the Danube.

Through all his vast domain, warm welcome thence
In such good haste as each could best devise,
To join the King at Shushan with their wives,
Their guards, their households, and their retinues
To eat and drink and make their hearts all glad
On the unstinted bounty of the king ;—
To centre the whole empire in a camp
Enjoying entertainments and delights
Even for the full space of a half a year
Nor dull one sense unto satiety.

From banks of Nile and coast of Araby,
And from beyond the rocky Sinjar cliffs
And the Assyrian cities of the plain,
From the Judean hills and Syrian vales,
From Nubian fastnesses and Libyan wastes,
From fallen Babylon and distant Ind,
From the gem islands of Ægean Sea—
From all the tributaries of the realm,
Within brief space, responsive to the call,
The chiefs and rulers of the tribes and states,
Their servants, families, and men-at-arms,
Were journeying toward Shushan, and in course
Within four months, the latest caravan
And cavalcade had drawn up at the gate
Of the king's palace and been duly welcomed.

When all had rested well and been restored
From weariness of travel, there was set,
By order of the king, a day when all
The provinces and tribes, by chosen troops
Appropriately mounted, duly armed,
Distinctly uniformed and panoplied,
Should thro' the streets of Shushan make parade
In honor of the king and the occasion
And the assembled guests, in such a pageant—
Such an array of various types of men—
Such a parade of nations, as the world
Had ne'er before, nor ever since hath, seen.

At rise of sun on the auspicious day,
All Shushan woke with glad expectancy
To witness the impressing spectacle,
And as a banner in the van unfurled,
A hundred trumpets flung their brazen tones
Upon the air ; and sixscore chiefs, and seven,
Threw into line their several cavalcades,
And then one trumpet-peal borne down the line
And taken up at reg'lar intervals
Was carried back a half score leagues until
The mighty concourse, summoned to advance,
Moved slowly forward. Carried at its head,
A short space in advance, fixed to a rod

Crossed on the shaft of a gold-pointed spear
And held aloft by a colossal Mede,   ·
Who sate a great white charger strong and proud
In his bejewelled harness, *Kaweianee*—
The leather apron of the mighty blacksmith—
The Standard Royal of the Persian State
Since time of Feridoon,—studded with gems
And trimmed with golden fringe, shone gorgeously
In the bright morning sun.   Next came the King.
Seated in state in a resplendent tow'r
Upon the back of a huge elephant—
Whose milk-white tusks were clasped with bands of gold,
And on occasion hung with tinkling bells,
And whose vast bulk richly caparisoned
With costly stuffs, all trimmed in filigree
Of gold and silver deftly interwoven,
Well symboled kingly power and boundless riches—
Moving in triumph and great majesty.
Then came the " Seven Princes " who might sit
Next to the King—his trusted counsellors—
And the three greatest captains of the realm—
The ten first personages in the empire—
Mounted alike on two great elephants—
(Five upon each) that moved on side by side,
Twins in their size and their caparisons,
Betokening the Persia-Median power ;

And on an outer perch, builded upon
The outer sides of their two gorgeous towers
Sat a gigantic Ethiop, black as night—
Immovable as carven ebony ;
And each one held aloft an ebon staff
Tipped with a silver star, the star enclosed
Within a wingéd circle of fine gold—
This last the symbol of Ahura Mazda,
The good and all-wise god,—and from these staffs
In shimmering silken folds floated in air
Twin banners of the empire.

After these—
The great king's special pride, tithe of his guard—
A thousand, matchless, strong, and godlike men—
Five hundred Persians and five hundred Medes,
The flower of all the realm, rode gallantly,
The first on coal-black steeds with archéd necks
Armored with flakes of brass half overlapped,
Their saddles of white leather, silver trimmed,
O'er scolloped blankets, worked with threads of gold ;
Their bridles made of silken cord and hung
With a white silken tassel 'neath the ear,
The front embellished with a silver star ;
The Medes on milk-white chargers sleek and strong,
Of the famed Nissæan breed, and panoplied

In all ways as the Persians' horses were,
Save in the color,—all things being black
In contrast with the steeds.

These thousand men,—
The Persians clad in a rich, armored garb,
Crossed, gilded harnesses, and bright steel helmets
All open-faced below, the upper front
Bossed with the wingéd circle deftly wrought ;
Each with a jewelled dagger in his girdle,
And a keen sword of wondrous workmanship,
Their glittering blades all damaskeened with gold,
And hilts inlaid with pearl and precious gems ;
The Medes, in dark cuirasses, greaves and boots,
And jewelled sashes, and all helmeted
With pointed casques emblazoned at the brow
With a half-risen sun of sheeny gold,
Whose inlaid rays spread out and upward, so
Pointing a golden arch upon the steel,
And armed with jewelled swords, and polished spears,
With shafts of cornel wood of matchless finish,—
In truth did seem a martial company ;
Clear-visaged, olive-skinned, and mustachioed,
Strong-limbed, deep-chested, sitting well their steeds,—
The boast and pleasure of the populace.

A company of white-skinned, stalwart Greeks,
Whose well-knit frames betokened rugged strength,
Followed the Medes, in lead of their own prince,
Who oft had led them in the deadly fray.
Over their heads the banner that they loved,—
The standard of their island, sea-girt home,
Bearing in woven gold an arméd Mars,—
Waved proudly. Finely horsed on steeds
That oft had borne their riders into battle ;
Armed with long spears, and maces, helmeted,
And clad in steel-bright armor, well they seemed
A valiant, warlike band.

Next after these,
Five hundred Indian bowmen, with their bows
And well-filled quivers o'er their shoulders thrown—
Five bowmen in a group, a hundred groups—
Sate in a hundred open-sided towers,
Borne by a hundred well trained elephants
Ranked side by side in fives as they passed on
In brilliant trappings, moving pond'rously,
With steady, well timed gait, all keeping step,
Their sinewy trunks swaying from side to side,
Their tusks—great pointed beams of ivory—
Like levelled lances in each massive rank,

Held ever ready for resistless charge,
While, gleaming from each elephantine front,
Shone a pale silver star, and over all,
From each alternate rank, waving on high,
The sun-kissed, golden banner of the Ind
Floated in air.

                            Now from Sweet Araby
Two hundred dwellers in the desert came,
On tall, brown camels (that with high-held heads
And swinging pace strode solemnly along)
Mounted, each on a fleshy pinnacle
Capped with a richly trimmed, fantastic seat,
Half saddle and half howdah, which they sate
At high-kneed stride in shifty attitude,
Their lithe forms clad in half-loose drapery,
Their crimson bonnets covering in part
Their swarthy cheeks, while each one held at rest,
Skyward aslant, a long, bright-pointed lance
Tasselled with colored streamers on the shaft
Just 'neath the glittering steel. Four hundred more
Of these swart sons of Araby, arrayed
And armed as were the cameliers,—save that,
At the right side of each, in jewelled sheath,
Hung a keen, crooked sword, with hilt of gold,—
Bestrode four hundred steeds as beautiful

As they were fleet,—as fleet as morning light ;
As true as tireless,—tireless as the wind ;
As gentle as courageous,—without fear ;
Their proud heads carried well on arching necks,
Their ready ears tilting for ev'ry sound,
Their half transparent nostrils drinking in
The life and vigor of the morning air,
Their clear, bold eyes obstructed by no blind,
Their shining, well groomed coats, like new-born fur,
Speaking the purest strain of desert barbs,
Their clean, sound, sinewy limbs and supple joints
Traced with a network of rich-blooded veins,
Their clear, firm hoofs unmarred by nail or shoe,
As hard and firm as blocks of adamant ;
And so they moved with measured, flexile step,
These twice two hundred steeds, which but a word—
One guiding impulse from their masters all—
Might change into a living hurricane,—
A many-splintered, rushing thunderbolt,
Flaming with banners, glittering with steel.

A hundred skilled Assyrian chariotiers,
With each an arméd archer at his side,
All clad in shining mail, and borne along
In gilded chariots, followed after these ;
Each chariot drawn by two impatient steeds—

Powerful stallions, eager and well fed—
Caparisoned even as in time of war
In armored housings : champing brazen bits
In fierce restraint, with their wild eyes ablaze,
And tossing angrily their heads in air,
They seemed as if athirst to dash away
And drag the murderous chariot scythes among
Some unseen hostile host.   As of this band,
Four hundred mounted spearmen followed on,
Both men and beasts magnificent in strength,
And in accoutrements, and trained to war ;—
Of such, as in the days long past had made
Assyria's name a dread and a reproach
Unto the nations.

        Chaldea next in line,—
Five hundred sons of fallen Babylon
Moved proudly on, their jewelled, polished arms,
Their flashing armor, and fleet-footed steeds
Caparisoned in trappings trimmed with gold,
Reflected still the grandeur of their state
And splendor of their once proud capitol.
Gaily they rode along, while o'er their heads
The Persian banners waved above their own
Borne side by side : And after these there came
Sad and dejected and of downcast mien

A mounted troop of the oft-times dispersed—
Remnant of Israel from far Palestine,—
Captor, and captive, in the conq'ror's train
Thus rode along.

　　　　A troop of Syrian horse
From distant Tadmor's desert-bounded walls
Followed at Israel's heels ; and after these
A company of Damascan cameliers
Mounted on two-hunched bactrians ;
And then there passed, in the imposing line,
A troop of Phœnicians from the coast
Of shell-paved Ægean ; and followed these,
The wonder of that truly wondrous train,
A band of belted bowmen, yellow-skinned,
Lithe-limbed and pouting-lipped, all richly clad,
In fitting hauberks mailed with links of gold,
Sandals, and quilted turbans feather-plumed,
And borne in chariots drawn by fiery steeds,
And blazoned with gilt figures—ibises,
And bulls and crocodiles—of things revered
In Pharaoh's land of monoliths and tombs.
Egypt's contingent this : the kingliest troop
Of all that cavalcade of kingly men ;
And as they passed, driv'n by their chariotiers,
'Neath banners blazoned with the asp and scarab,

The head of Amun and the Sun's broad disk,
They leaned upon their bows, gazed straight ahead,
And seemed to think of naught save that past time
When Egypt led the world, nor ever thought
That she might one day grace a conq'ror's pageant.
Five hundred fierce Caducians (from the north,
Beyond the Caspian Gates,) renowned in war
And dextrous with the deadly javelin,
Came after Egypt on their tireless steeds,
In light fur tunics clad ; their coarse, wild hair
Trimmed to a central tussock on the crown,
Their dark brows wound about with purple cloth
Pinned with the hookéd claws of savage beasts;
Hard-visaged, savage men, cruel yet brave,
Armed with their fav'rite weapon, and with bows,
And ready arrows quivered at their backs,
Guiding their chargers with a single rein.

Then came a band of Asiatic Scyths,—
A troop from that vast horde that roamed at will
North of the Oxus, reaching to the banks—
And yet beyond—of broad Jaxartes stream,
A company of wild barbaric men
Mounted superbly, armed with only bows
And feathered arrows, fitted with bronze heads,

Which, dipped in subtle poison, are winged death
Sped by these matchless bowmen in fierce battle.

And after these the Parthian heavy horse,
Five hundred strong—a troop of giant men—
Mounted on powerful steeds, strong-limbed and tall,
And horse and rider clad in rugged mail
Of overlapping scales of hammered iron.
Each rider wore a burnished iron casque,
Surmounted by a golden blaze-like point,
Upon his head, and in his strong right hand,
Balanced at rest, he bore a pond'rous spear,
While with his left he guided his good steed ;
And so, ten in each rank, they moved along,
A living wall of rugged strength and power,
While from the centre of each seventh rank,
Borne high upon a tasselled, cross-barred staff,
Floated their standard of the rising sun.
Next came Armenians, and next Lydians came,
And so troop followed troop until there passed
A company from every separate tribe
And province in the whole far-reaching empire ;
Three continents in one long line of march—
A stream of waving banners, glittering arms,
And men of martial bearing borne along

On elephants, and camels, horses, chariots,
Till lastly, bringing up the distant rear,
A troop of stalwart, coal-black Ethiops,
Nude, save a short skirt round their ebon loins,
Bands of white ivory about their arms
And snow-white plumes upon their turbaned heads,
Came into view like a dark cloud of war ;
And each one bore an ivory-pointed spear
With a long, slender shaft of polished cane,
Carried at level poise in his right hand,
Upon his forearm, prest against his side.
On dark brown steeds well seated, ten abreast,
And fifty deep, and every man in line,
These dusky warriors and their hardy mounts
Beneath barbaric banners moved along.

Under the stately palms, outside the gates,
Hard by the palace in an open space
Sloping toward the walled course of Chaospes,
Upon a dais, on a gilded throne
Approached by rows of cushioned seats like steps
One o'er the other, and extending out
A distance right and left, the mighty King,
Now having quit the great procession, sate.
Behind him stood the royal fan-bearer
And holder of the royal parasol,

Each at his duty, and on either side
A dozen tried and trusty men-at-arms
Magnificently armored and equipped ;
While ranged below upon the sloping ground
And facing outward in ten open ranks,
And in each rank a thousand chosen men
Extending right and left before the throne,
Stood the King's body-guard, the famed IMMORTALS,[1]
In armored hauberks and tall, pointed casques
Of steel, becrested with a wingéd disk
Of hammered gold, and each on his left arm,
At level rest, upheld an oblong shield
Of plated brass, and with his mailed right hand,
Close by his side, held his keen-pointed spear,
Clasped by its polished shaft of cornel wood,
The round butt planted firmly near his foot,
The hand-holt wound about with golden wire,
And the bright two-edged head reaching above

[1] The "Immortals" were a corps of 10,000 chosen foot-soldiers, carefully selected from among the Medes and Persians only, and maintained by all the early Persian monarchs as a body-guard, taking their name from the fact that, notwithstanding deaths or removals from other causes, the ranks were immediately refilled, and so the number, 10,000, continuously maintained. The "Immortals" of the great Xerxes are said to have been among the first troops in the assault at Thermopylae, and at that time to have been almost exterminated by Leonidas and his Greeks.

2

The golden crest upon his shining helmet ;
So seemed they a long bank of brazen shields
Stubbled with lances, like a harvest glebe,
Glorious with shining crests and waving banners ;
While nearer to the King, upon the seats
On either side of him, and yet below,
Sate tributary rulers, satraps, kings,
High officers of state and counsellors
All in their courtly robes, there to behold
The wondrous, arméd pageant of the nations.
And each one viewed with pride, as it passed by,
The troop of his own land, and heard with joy
The populace send up its mighty shout
Of cordial greeting.

        Following on this,
After the great procession, in the eve,
The King threw open to his noble guests
The portals of his palace, great Shushan,
That they might feast their eyes upon its splendors
And there behold on his imperial throne,
Seated in royal state, the King himself,
In his great majesty, to welcome them,
And entertain them even as he willed
According to his pleasure. So the women,
In a like manner, Vashti, the fair Queen,

Even at the royal house, would take in charge
To give them pleasure with her gracious smiles,
The clear, sweet music of her sisters' harps
And sweeter tones from their yet sweeter lips
Uniting music and soft dulcet speech
Into seraphic song.

As night drew on,
And daylight faded out, the pale, dim stars,
Only half seen at first, one here, one there,
Yonder a little group, a cluster still
Directly overhead, timidly showed themselves
Just on night's threshold ; but soon growing bold
The countless astral worldlets stepping forth
Into the open sky, decked its blue dome
With gems of wondrous lustre.

The outer court,
And royal grounds about the Great King's palace,—
The trees, along the walks and avenues
And in the groves, and round the pebbly pools,
Were hung with lanterns shedding various lights,
Red, green, and blue, all colors of the bow,
And intermediate tints, till all the park
Like a vast plot set with tall flow'ring plants
Shone in the night all luminous with blooms

That on the lakelets glanced their wondrous beams
Where white swans sailed among the mirrored stars.

Within the palace, in the circled hall—
The throne-room builded by the Great Darius—
A thousand silver lamps with chains of gold,
Hung from the high arched ceiling of blue sapphire,
Lit with their flaming cressets, the mock sky
Studded with brilliants, like the constellations,
To represent the heavenly firmament,
(The joint production of Chaldean science
And the constructive art of gifted Greece.)
And this was horizoned with plates of pearl
Whose wat'ry tints shone like an opal sea
In wavy lines of inter-melting shade.

Around the drap'ried walls, reaching beyond
The circling pillars of the royal dome
In all ways save the rear ; from pedestal,
And bracket, and pilastered niche, looked out
Many a graven image of white marble,
And polished ivory, and gilded wood,
With form and features of great heroes past,
Of celebrated warriors, gifted sages,
Of foreign gods and personated virtues—
Chiselled in swelling bust and full-length statue.

And many were the spoils of Persia's wars,
And some had grown beneath the magic touch
Of Canachus and those who with him strove
With first success to wed Art unto Nature
In closest semblance ; yet who sought to clothe
The Arts and Virtues, and the gods of Greece
In human form, forever yet Divine
And most suggestive to the human heart,
And, so, most claiming human sympathy
And reverential worship.

                Toward the rear,
And facing the broad, polished, brazen gate
Of the main entrance to the great rotunda,
Upon his golden throne, whose lion feet
Pressed on a platform of the whitest marble
Approached by marble steps, and at the pave
On either side flanked by a wingéd monster,
Half human and half beast, of carven stone,
The King Ahasuerus sate. On either side
Near to the throne there crouched a gilded lion,
And o'er his head there arched a canopy
Of finest Indian silk, befringed with gold,
Upheld by golden posts, and 'broidered o'er
With battle scenes and pictures of the chase.
A score of armored spearmen on the steps—

Two upon each in facing, rising lines—
Thus guarded the approach unto the King
From wingéd sphynxes to the golden throne ;
And when the noble guests had entered in
To the great circled chamber of the throne
With its tall fluted pillars ranged around
With curtains op'ning into flanking halls,
Each did prostrate himself before the King,
Who then arose, outstretched the golden sceptre,
Bade all arise, then took one forward step,
And spake his greeting thus :
                    " Kings, satraps, princes !
Chieftains, wise men of state, and counsellors !
May joy attend you as our welcome doth
In this our capitol and palace Shushan.
And further still, in this behalf, pray you,
Accept our royal thanks, in that ye came
So promptly to us at our instance here
(Proving full well your love and loyalty),
That we might see you all, and speak with you
Concerning various matters of our realm
Wherein we all have common interest ;
So, too, ye meet ourself, and one another,
And so, each knowing all, all knowing each !
We may the better for our glorious empire
Take common counsel and united action

Should the occasion come, and thus prepared,
With the just sanction of the immortal gods
We shall be able still, as we have been,
To well uphold, or even to extend
The wise dominion of our common realm.
One thing provokes our wrath as may it yours—
The arrogance of the Athenians,
Who since they 'scaped destruction at the hands
Of our majestic father, great Darius,
And through the intervention of their gods
Obtained the victory at Marathon,
Have grown so mighty in their own esteem,
And yet withal so blunt, so insolent,
And so defiant of our Persian power
As well to earn chastisement.   Sparta, too,
Is contumacious, and with other states
Beyond the Ægean, may make common cause
With these most boastful men of Attica—
These braggart burners of our city, Sardis,[1]
And so oppose our arms with no mean force ;
Yet, the more sure shall be their overthrow,
By your good service, when the time shall come.

[1] During the Ionian revolt an expedition was led against Sardis in which the Athenians joined, during the reign of Darius. The expedition " had taken Sardis—it had burned one of the chief cities of the Great King."—Rawlinson's *An. Mon.*, vol. ii., p. 482.

After the term of our festivities
And the full season of due preparation,
Then shall the mightiest host that man e'er saw—
The embattled force of all our provinces,
A multitude whose tread shall shake the hills—
Tramp under foot our boastful enemies
To the great glory of our whole domain
To whose most splendid seat ye now are come
To be awhile our guests, partake our cheer,
And look upon our glory, and your own,
Vouchsafed us by the gods. Welcome again !
Be happy and content ! "

                                  So having said,
The King resumed his seat upon the throne
And stretching out before him his right hand
He waved the golden sceptre to'ard the throng
Denoting thus that he who would might speak
For all, or for himself.
                              Then stepping forth,
One claiming kin with great Nebuchadnezzar
(Whose fame and greatness once had filled the earth)
And King of Babylon by sufferance—
Dividing rule with a cold Persian satrap
Appointed by great Xerxes for his wisdom,
His firmness, and his Zoroastrian zeal—

Bowed very low and then addressed the throne
Speaking for self and all the company,
And thus :
  " O, King of Kings, live on forever !
Reign ever whilst thou livest, and be happy !
When thou dost speak, the nations list and heed,
For like unto thee upon all the earth
There is not one, for glorious majesty,
For power, for feats of arms, for mighty deeds,
For wealth in goods, and wisdom in thy words,
Thou art above all others save the gods
In strength to overcome thine enemies
And to uphold thy friends ! Thy subjects we,
Rulers by thee, and for thee, in thy stead,
From all the more than hundred provinces
Of thy far-reaching, and most glorious realm,
Have come before thee here at thy behest
Feeling much honored ; and we pledge thee here
On bended knees, before thy kingly throne,
Our trusty faith and deathless fealty,
Our heart's blood and the full strength of our arms
In the upholding of thy matchless empire
And the chastisement of thine enemies,
Come whence they may, or if thou go to them,
In the extending further of thy sway
Over the world that knows thee not as yet

As King above all others.   Furthermore,
O King ! extend unto thy Queen, our Queen,
The fair and faultless Vashti (whom we love
For her great virtues as we love our mothers),
Our reverential homage and our prayers.
Dismiss thy servant, he has had his say."

How was the haughty humbled ! Babylon,
Whose fierce imperious pride once could have brooked
Naught but submission to her own behests—
Whose learning was the treasure of the world—
Whose art had reared on high the world's fourth
    wonder—
Who from her massive walls and brazen gates
Had mocked and sneered defiance at the nations—
Babylon, who, bitter and merciless,
Had dragged her conquered to captivity,
Or given them, disarmed, unto the sword,
With insolent taunts of the fine privilege
Of being slaughtered by so great a power—
How abject was she now, praising her chains
And glorifying him who kept them locked
About her once free limbs ;—a sycophant,
Mouthpiece of sycophants, who under stress
Proclaim their own abasement.
                                    Babylon

Being dismissed, the King called his musicians,
The singers of the court, the psalterers,
Harpers, and those who play the mellow lute,
To come before his majesty and sing
And play before his august company—
His guests assembled ; and they came and stood
A goodly company and all trained singers,
One from each tribe and nation, till they told
More than a hundred nations of the realm,
And standing there four deep, they raised their voices,
And strumming to themselves accomp'niment
Sang with a wondrous volume and rich cadence
Thus, to the assembled nations :

SONG OF THE NATIONS.

" Come sounding from the Memphian tombs
  The triumphs of the Pharaohs ;
Comes echoing from the Tyrian looms
  The tale of how Phœnicia rose ;
The rebuilt temple courts the sun
Whose glory shone on Solomon
  And on Judea's woes.

" Still Babylon's wondrous splendor dwells
  Within her brazen gates and halls ;

Assyria her greatness tells
From Nineveh's half-buried walls;
The old-time fame of Araby
Comes breathing o'er her deserts free
In incense-laden calls.

"Of old the mighty Indus spread
    The prestige of the Indian name ;
The Nile tells how Sabaco led
    His Ethiopians down to fame ;
Proud Baalbec's mighty temple sings
The fiery song of Syria's kings
    Which glory fans to flame.

"A hundred voices of the sea
    Speak of proud Grecia's hundred isles,
Her art and her philosophy,
    And from Ionia's splendid piles
The cunning of her builders' hands
Hath shed its light in many lands
    Like to the sun-god's smiles.

"The Lydian streams o'er golden sands
    Flow murm'ring to the list'ning sea,
Telling where glorious Sardis stands
    Proud of her fame and history.

Armenia's ark-famed mountain peak [1]
And Bactria's lofty banners [2] speak :
'The pride of heroes we.'

" Now all the glories that we sing
Of all the glorious nations named
Unite in thy great realm, O King,
And all the fame of all the famed
'Mong nations, neath thy royal crown,
Is heightened by a wide renown
More than each erst had known.

" Sits Persia on her tabled plains
A goddess 'mong the nations fair
O'er which Ahasuerus reigns,
And lo, the nations gathered here
Before great Xerxes' golden throne
Behold a glory half their own
That Persia loves to share."

[1] Ararat.

[2] " Bactria was a country which enjoyed the reputation of having
been great and glorious at a very early date. In one of the most
ancient portions of the Zendavesta it was celebrated as ' *Bakhdi*
eredhwo drofsha ' or ' Bactria with the lofty banner.' "—Rawlinson,
Seven Great Monarchies, vol. ii., p. 440.

After the song, and sev'ral melodies
In which the hundred joined with instruments,
In a sweet wilderness of chording sounds
A company of dancing girls were called,
Gazelle-eyed Persian maids and fair-haired Greeks,
Damsels, with eyes of night, from famed Meroe,
Egypta's full-lipped daughters, lovely Medes,
Fair Scythian slave-girls, captive Jewesses,
Lithe Indian maidens, graceful as wild swans,—
A sprightly band, as beautiful as nymphs,
With willowy forms and finely rounded limbs ;
They came before the royal company
And to the notes of lute and clarionet
Danced with a sylph-like grace, and as they danced
The pearls that hung about their necks in strings
Lay milky-white upon their heaving breasts ;
Their anklet bells tinkled a tiny rhythm,
Their jewelled arms flashed in the mazy whirl,
Heightening the charm of youth on their flushed cheeks,
And their bright eyes shone with a witching light,
While scarce their feet appeared to touch the floor,
So did their warm young spirits seem absorbed,
And they so buoyed, by the enchanting spell
Of music-prompted motion. Forming at length
In a wide circle, hand in hand they moved
With motions similar and steps well timed,

Then broke in single line and disappeared
Whence they had come.
           Now, after these had gone,
A company of giants, huge and tall,
One each, from all the nations, strode along
And formed before the throne a crescent line
Saluting all, the King ; and lo, there stood
On the extended, open palm of each,
On the right side, a dwarf of the same tribe,
Clad and accoutred e'en as was the wont
Of the true warriors of their sev'ral tribes ;
And thus was represented the armed power
And the upholding strength of all the realm
Hedging about the Great King, on his throne,
Before the gathered nations. Then the dwarfs
Leaped from the giants' palms unto the pave
And formed into a square, and there performed
The warlike evolutions of trained troops
Of all the various tribes, each being trained
In all the various movements of the others,
All going through the whole in unison
With wonderful precision. Then all bowed
And marched from view. The brawny giants then
Exhibited feats of prodigious strength,
Each one excelling in some special sense
And gaining plaudits from the company ;

And when all quit at length the royal presence
A gray-beard Indian juggler came in view,
Bearing a bamboo wand, tipt with a star—
A star emitting a most wondrous light,
Yet not, as it might seem, fixed to the wand,
And made of polished metal, glit'ring gem,
Or any substance that men understood,
But an effulgent spot with pointed rays
Spreading in all ways from the radiant centre
And clinging like a magnet to the tip
Of that plain, simple reed, and resting there
When e'er the wand was still, and when not so,
Then chasing after, like as doth a shadow
Follow a substance in the shining sun ;
And as he stood beneath an archéd passage
He seemed a moment to be lost in thought,
Then made a low obeisance to the King
And to the royal guests, then waved his wand,
With a slow, circling motion, in the air,
When lo ! there stood before him, in an instant,
Coming no one knew whence, or how, or why,
A dozen tawny men, some young, some old,
All seeming by their garb and subtle movements
To be of the same calling with the first,
And they did there perform such wondrous feats,
Such arts of magic, cunning conjurings,

And dextrous tricks, astonishing eye and ear,
As quite surprised, as well as entertained
And mystified all who beheld.
                          At length,
Again the gray-beard wizard waved his wand
And stamped his foot, and lo ! he was alone.
Then bowing low once more before the King,
He cast his eyes about him and above,
And with his star-tipped reed waved once again,
Telling a circle slowly through the air,
Then uttered a few strange, mysterious words,
At which a half score vaguely outlined shapes
Enshrouded in white vapor, and illumed
With all the thousand lamps that hung above,
Moved, floating in mid-air above the pave
Till in the central space before the throne,
Then rested ; when the mist part cleared away,
Revealing—now reclining on a cloud,
In miniature, that lay in fleecy banks
Beneath them, and about their naked feet—
A semicircle of the loveliest forms,
And faces the most beautiful to view
That men on earth did ever look upon,—
Bright-eyed and glorious-haired, ripe-limbed
And ruby-lipped, a lovely company—
A band of Peris yet awhile detained
3

From the celestial fields of Paradise
(Sweet innocency and seraphic smiles
Lighting their beauteous faces), summoned here,
A spectacle before the wondering nations ;
And while all looked and marvelled, moving back,
Waving his mystic wand, the sorcerer
Slowly withdrew, bowing himself from sight ;
And as he did so those fair virgin forms
Slowly dissolved from view, faded away,
Until it seemed the space where they had lain
Recumbent in the air was twice more vacant
Than all the empty space surrounding it.
Thus with diversions various and strange
Did the great King contrive to please his guests
Throughout the evening hours ; and so for months,
Day after day, and night succeeding night,—
With state ceremonials or imposing pageant,
Some musical rehearsal, priestly rite
(Wherein each people worshipped as they would
According to their several beliefs
And 'stablished customs, serving their own gods),
Some wondrous feats of supple acrobats,
Wild dances and resplendent pantomimes,
Displays of horsemanship by the lithe Arabs,
The nomad Scyths, and agile Parthians
All mounted on their best-trained, swiftest steeds ;

Wrestling among the athletes of the tribes
Of the whole empire ; trials of rude strength,
And friendly tournaments and jousts at arms,—
Were the hours filled with rounds of joy and pleasure ;
Beside the feastings and the merry-makings
That for the time made Shushan the chief mart
And capitol of pleasure of the world.

And now for six bright merry months, the sun
Had shone on Shushan as a glorious camp
Of nations gathered to make holiday
As the invited guests of the great monarch ;
So, ere all took departure for their homes
The King proclaimed an universal feast
To all within his city, great and small,
For seven days, in the broad garden court
Of his great palace, 'mid most dazzling splendors ;
And all the open court where they did feast
Was paved in cunning patterns with fine marble,
Black, white, and red, and blue, all intermixed,
And laid to the design with wondrous skill,
While round about, tall and magnificent,
Rose fluted columns of white porphyry
Spanned with light, airy arches of the same,
Keyed with the tapering necks of double griffins,
Whose sturdy heads, faced right and left aloft,

Formed short pilasters for a carven cornice ;
And 'twixt the columns stretched fine linen cords,
Pale blue and purple, looped o'er hooks of gold,
And from the cords, on burnished silver rings,
Hung fairy clouds of textile handiwork—
Damaskan hangings, curtains from Kashmir,
Rich silks in patterns from the Indian looms,
Fine textiles wrought in Babylon and Tyre,
Rare stuffs in green, and gold, and blue, and white,
Caught back between the pillars here and there
In folds of shimmering lustre, and made fast
O'er golden roses set on silver stems
Fixed in the columns' shafts ; while all within
Were scores of playing fountains ranged about
Spurting their cooling waters high in air ;
And here and there a clump of stately palms
Surrounded by a lovely bit of sward,
Roses in bloom, and clumps of greenery
Like sweet oases in a marble desert,
Smiled Nature's smile, there, in the midst of Art.
And all the beds whereon the guests reclined
While at the royal board, were of fine woods,
All richly carven, inlaid with fine gold
And holstered with rare textiles and bright furs,
And every guest was giv'n a golden cup—
Each dif'ring from the rest—wherefrom he drank

Wine, from the royal vintage, rare and old,
Crushed from the luscious grapes of sunny Helbon ;
And every one did drink e'en as he listed,
None urging, none withholding, but all free,
Till on the seventh and last day of the banquet,
The King, being full merry with much wine,
And so warmed by the gen'rous drink, and all
His senses dulled to strict propriety,
And in his heart desiring much that Vashti—
Whom graciously the people reverenced—
Should come before the assembled company
(Now merry in their cups and full of speech),
Unveiled, wearing the royal crown and robes,
That all the people there, might thus behold
Her wondrous beauty and sweet queenly grace,
Ordered his chamberlains to summon her
Thus to the kingly presence and forthwith ;
Closing the hasty order to them thus :
" Tell her the King awaits her !   Let her come ! "

And so they went and did the king's command,
And Vashti, knowing of the flow of wine
Among the thousands feasting with the King,
And being busied with her own fair guests,
Was much amazed to hear the king's behest,
And thinking surely there was some mistake

Went not, but told the chamberlains to come
Yet once again, were 't still the king's desire,
And she would hasten to him. So they did
And came before the King, when cold Harbona,
With fixed, immobile face, while bowing down
Thus spake their message to Ahasuerus :
" O King, live thou forever ! Thy fair queen
Bade us repair to thee, and say to thee :
If this thing be thy wish unalterable
To send us once again, and she will come
In haste to do thy bidding, dutiful
In full obedience."

                Then the King with rage
Grew red, and stamped his foot and swore an oath :
" By great Cambyses' sword ! Am I defied
In my own household ? and by my own queen ? "
Then turning fiercely on the chamberlains
He ordered them away but not to Vashti ;
And when he had in measure quieted
The storm of passion raging in his soul
He spake unto the wise men who sat near—
The seven princes first in all the realm
In the King's favor, and his counsellors—
Saying : " According to the law, of right
What should be done to our rebellious queen

Who thus hath set at naught our just commands
In presence of our realm, here represented
By our illustrious guests convened at Shushan ? "
And Memucan, most forward of the seven
And readiest in expedient and speech,
Made answer to the King, and thus :

      " O King !
Vashti the queen hath done most grievous wrong
In this her stiff-necked disobedience,
And not to thee alone, but unto all
Thy princes, and all men throughout the realm ;
For this deed of the queen shall go abroad
On eagles' wings and speak with clam'rous tongues,
So that all women soon shall hear of it,
And shall despise their husbands ; even so
Our ladies here in Persia, Media,
Shall treat thy princes, hearing of this deed.
If this thing go unpunished, unrebuked,
Who, of the countless husbands in the land
Shall after this hold sway in his own house?
Or if some may by dint of self-assertion
Manage to govern still in their own homes,
Yet were it true, the queen hath this day sown
The seeds of such domestic bickerings,
Mockings, denials of authority,

Railings, dissimulations, and contempts,
As in their springing up and noxious growth
Will smother quiet peace and harmony
And blossom with dissensions, spleen and wrath
And all confusions. Now, O King,
If it so please thee, let it be decreed
As thy commandment royal, and be writ
Among our laws, that it may not be changed,
That Vashti come no more before the King ;
And do thou give away her whole estate
And her insignia of royalty
Unto another worthier than she ;
So, when thou hast commanded and decreed
And published the decree throughout the realm,
All wives shall yield obedience to their husbands
And duly honor them."

      The King seemed pleased
With these suggestions of fierce Memucan,
And being stayed, and their cool reason checked
By the hot torrent of his sounding words
No other prince did raise his voice against it ;
And so the King proclaimed, e'en as advised,
With many else severe particulars,
And so decreed against the youthful queen,
And all was written down among the laws
Of Media and Persia, by the scribes.

Then went there criers through the city Shushan,
And couriers post-haste thro' all the realm
To publish what was writ, in many tongues,
To make it understood 'mong all the people.

Next day the King did call the eunuchs in—
Even the seven trusty chamberlains,
And as they waited near on bended knees
Cowering before the King's still blazing wrath
He spake unto them saying :
                  "Slaves, attend !
Go to the woman Vashti ! Our decree
Fail not to execute, but carry out
Even to the very letter as 't is writ !
Rid her of all her goods ! Rid me of her !
This palace rid of disobedience !
The law is your instruction ! Now be gone !"

So they went forth into the women's house
And in a half hour's course came Mehuman—
One of the seven, noted for his great strength,
Kindness of heart, and never-daunted courage—
Again before the King, and stood there pale
As marble statue, and he seemed as calm.
Then, bowing low at first, stood up erect
And spake unto the King whose cloudy brow

Frowned fiercely on him as he said and thus :
" O King, pardon thy humblest slave, or let
Thy vengeance smite him, as thou seest fit,
For from my heart the queen did wring a promise
To come to thee and say : ' *Ahasuerus, King*
Of Persia, Media, and the provinces
Did promise unto Vashti his young queen
Upon her nuptial day, that any wish
She then did have, or after might express,
E'en to the granting of one half his kingdom,
Should not be made in vain ! And now the queen
Doth humbly beg of him to stretch his hand
Forth with the golden staff that she may come
To speak her wish before him, and to shew
The innocency of her breaking heart
Plainly unto him.' "—Purpling with wild rage
Thus brake the King upon him :
      " Daring knave !
Emasculated worm ! Mutinous wretch !
How durst thou stand and look me in the face
And speak to me of given promises ?
Go tell the woman that the thing she says
Was spoken to the queen ! She is not such,
But a banned outcast ! Go, mad fool !
Do as thou 'rt bid ; and know that on the morrow
Thy traitorous tongue that thus dared speak to me,

Shall be cut from thy mouth, and thy cold eyes
That dared look unabashed into my face
While thou didst speak thy treason, shall be made
That they may never so again offend."
So he who knew not fear, went forth in silence
To duty, and to doom, each worse than death.

BOOK II.

VASHTI.

A S rose the Summer sun above the plain
Stretching away to'ard the Sargatian desert,
In a lone outskirt of the city Shushan,
Beside a walled-in pool, beneath the shelter
Of some great palms that clustered round about
As if they too had come to quench their thirst
With the cool waters that they hedged around,
A woman young and fair, but with the seal
Of grief set deep upon her youthful face—
A woman in the coarse garb of disgrace
And deep humiliation, stooping, dipped
A gourd of water from the pool and drank ;
And when she 'd slaked her thirst she looked about,
Heaved a deep sigh, then gazed into the pool,
Saying : " This still is left ! I may come here
Even as the beggars do ; and if I haste
To come at early morn, I yet may drink

Without disturbing any other soul
With my shunned, dreaded presence ; and the Sun—
O Mithra ! in the glory of thy rising,
I still may look upon and worship thee,
As being the best gift of the all-wise
And all-beneficent Ahura Mazda
To everything that lives upon the earth ;
And the sweet, balmy air, I breathe it still
And feast my eyes on Zagros' distant summits
With no one to forbid or hinder me ;
What else ? aye, what ? A morsel now and then,
A beggar's dole, given in fear or shame
Or mayhap both. And who am I that mourn
And wail my poor estate unto myself,
Scarce knowing if the things I see are real,
Or if the griefs I feel are actual,
Or if the words I utter yet have meaning
According to the import of plain speech ?
Since scarce I know if I be sane or mad.
And since how long ? a fortnight or a month ?
Or more than this, or less ? I cannot tell !
But it seems very long that I have suffered,
And yet so short a time since I was happy.

" Comparing what I was with what I am—
But yesterday I was a queen whose crown

Blazed with the glitter of a thousand gems
The choicest in a hundred provinces
Sent by a hundred tributary kings,
With flattering words to King Ahasuerus
And to myself, each begging that the stones
That each had sent might find an humble place
In my tiara. ' Vashti, the gracious queen ! '
' Vashti the beautiful, whom all revere ! '
' Vashti, whose virtues are on every tongue ! '
' Vashti, the star of thy most kingly court ! '
' Vashti, whose light is like the rising sun
Thro' all the kingdoms of thy mighty realm ! '
These and a hundred more of like import
Were honeyed messages the couriers brought
From all the chiefs and rulers far and near
In praise of Vashti. Media, Persia, sang
The praise of Vashti. No one save the King,
From Indus to the Ethiopian plains,
In all the tributaries of the realm
Had more of honors or emoluments.
Princes and mighty men did bring for me,
Laying them at the feet of the great King,
Rare gifts in great profusion of such kind
As was most perfect in their sev'ral lands,—
Incense and spices from far Araby
And horses fleet 's the wind, and beautiful

As morning light, and graceful as gazelles.
And came from Tyre rich store of royal purple,
Yield of her looms ; rare jewels of fine gold,
Clasping with tiny fingers deftly wrought
Gems like the stars of night for brilliancy,
And also thence came cunning furniture
Wrought from the cedar wood of Lebanon,
Perfumed in grain and fibre with sweet scents,
Inlaid with gold and pearl and ivory
And builded for my chambers.   From Kashmir,
And from great Babylon's and Borsippa's looms,
Rare shawls and costly stuffs, rich tapestries
And cloth of silver thread and woven gold
Fashioned in curious patterns and designs ;
Carpets and figured hangings and rare lace.
And from the jungles of the further East
Rich store of peltries—wondrous tiger skins
Whose tawny ground traversed with glossy bars
Of darker fur, are to the touch as down ;
Leopards' sleek coats, their clear-lined, ebon spots
Sprinkled at random on a field of gold,
And the soft yielding vestment of the ounce,
All painted by that glowing Indian sun
With dyes of beauty ; till my 'partments, draped
With rarest fabrics of the weaver's skill,
And carpeted with rugs that each had cost

Some jungle tyrant his ferocious life,
Were deemed a gorgeous wonder to behold ;
From those warm shores they also sent to me
Some beauteous bright-winged birds of paradise
And golden pheasants, trogans, promerops,
Until they thronged the outer groves of Shushan
And the tall trees that grace the open court
Near by the palace, which at times appeared
Abloom with life and color.   From the coast
Of Caspian, and distant western shores
They brought me store of amber and quaint shells ;
And agates from the desert.   From the South,
And from the tribute islands of the sea,
Opals and jaspars, sards, and turquoises,
Ambergris, and much goods of woven grass,
Rare strings of milk-white pearls, and pearls in bulk
Like winnowed seeds for plenty.   From the West
The choicest offerings of Syria
And distant Egypt.   So sent Palestine
Some golden relics from the house of God—
From David's city, e'en Jerusalem,
Part of King David's store, and Solomon's,
Broken and spoiled at the Captivity
Nor coming to Nebuchadnezzar's hand,
So not included in Great Cyrus's gift,
But of the remnant left in Israel

And being not restored were sent to me
As rich mementoes of a great event.

" Scarce hath a caravan from east, or west,
The plains and mountains north, or wave-washed
    shores
Of southmost Araby, come into Shushan
In these three years that hath not brought some gift
(With the consent of King Ahasuerus)
To Vashti with the master-merchant's words
Of loyal reverence, till my store hath been—
In all the realm produces, or the skill
Of all its peoples fashions cunningly—
Of great abundance, and enabled me
(Not drawing on the King's munificence
At all times royal and unlimited)
To live in splendor as befits a queen,
And give with hand unstinted, as I wished.
So all the women of the royal house,
My lovely sisters—wives unto the King—
Shared in my bounty, and returned my love ;
For surely I did love them as my soul,
And as I loved none other save the King,
And my heart's joy, my babe, now mine no more—
In all the world, that death has spared to me ;
And who could help but love them ? their sweet youth,
  4

The innocency of their guileless lives,
Their wondrous beauty, and their helplessness,
Their trusting natures and their pretty ways,
Alone, had won a colder heart than mine.
I loved them further that they loved the King,
Who took delight in their companionship
Next to my own ; and often in the court,
Or place in common of the women's house,
They gathered round me like a wall of flowers
And held their pretty lips up to be kissed,
And twined their soft arms round my neck and spake
Such tender words, so full of boundless love,
So laden with desire to please me well,
That, tho' I was as young as most of them,
I came to look upon the fairy nymphs
As my own children in reality,
As oft they called themselves in their sweet speech ;
And I would look upon them with a pride
Such as methinks a mother well might feel
In feasting her fond eyes on the fair forms
And fairer faces of her own sweet daughters
Grown to the first estate of womanhood
And yet still full of girlish playfulness.
Oft, too, with psaltery and tuneful lute
They played to give me joy, until the drops
Of glittering water thrown up from the jets

Of the surrounding, ever-playing fountains
Like showers of shining pearls, on their return
Into the fountain bowls of porphyry,
Seemed like the rhythmic falling of sweet sounds
Self-tuned and mingled into melody.
And some would raise their voices clear and soft
As balmy breezes wantoning o'er the strings
Of an else-untouched harp, and improvise,
At times, some little song to praise the queen ;
And in my desolation, even now
One of these little nothings to my lips
Springs all unbidden, and the irony
Of changed conditions gives to it a voice,
Of mocking bitterness, and yet its words
Do fascinate me in my misery,
And thus I seem to hear them in the air.

"VASHTI OUR QUEEN.

"'All hail, our lovely queen,
The first of women she,
Of whom no evil can be said,
To whom all Media bows the head
And Persia bends the knee.

"'In beauty unsurpassed,
Yet not so fair as good,

Queen of a hundred states and thrones
And loved of all, thy worth atones
All sins of womanhood.

" ' Our great King's life and love
Are centred in thy eyes,
For Vashti is the queenly star
Who lights the throne of Persia far,
As Orion lights the skies

" ' From Ethiopia's sands
To Indus's watery wall
Is Vashti's goodness as the rain
That falls upon the thirsty plain
A heritage to all.'

" What a strange commentary on my past
Would be the recitation of my present !
But I 've no need to speak my present state,
It is upon me visible to all,
And more apparent to myself than any ;
Others behold me but a little while,
One for a moment now, another then,
But to myself I always am in sight,
And should I wish to quite forget myself
And draw a veil of darkness o'er the past

Some finger will be raised at me in scorn,
Some voice will mutter ' Vashti,' dreaded name,
Which but to speak aloud will clear the ground—
Of ev'ry thing that 's human and can hear—
About me like a sudden thunderbolt
That threatens repetition where it falls.

" My fair young sisters of the women's house,
I never shall set eyes on them again !
No more shall I behold my little son,
Nor shall I ever look upon the King,
For when he goes abroad the streets are cleared
Or all unworthies against whom a ban
Of any sort hath been decreed and writ.
And the great palace, and the royal grounds
Are doubly guarded against such as I,
While those whose duty is not to repel,
Flee from me like the touch of pestilence.
The common people whom I always helped
In some way by a silent charity
Shrink from my presence with averted looks
And downcast faces. Bondsmen and rude slaves
Hold me beneath them. Beggars turn aside
As tho' I were contagion. Yesterday,
While wandering aimlessly, thoughtlessly, straying
Beyond the city's limits till I came,

Not knowing it, to some low wretched huts
Given over to the moving breathing dead,
A shrivelled leper, hideous with sores,
But chanced to hear my name, as I passed by
The little open area where he lay
Sunning the relics of his misery,
When, with a piteous groan, he crawled away,
Dragging his dead limbs after, in such haste,
With such a seeming agony of fear
Portrayed on his wild hopeless face, as he
Cast o'er his shoulder one despairing glance,
As filled my soul with horror. This poor wretch
In whose decaying frame besieging death
Mocked at the feeble garrison of life—
This poor and half-dead lump of loathsomeness,
Instead of fleeing with the cry ' *unclean* '
To warn against infection through himself,
Seemed terrified lest that my moral taint
Should spread upon the atmosphere he breathed
And, mingling with the humors of his flesh,
Thus work his quick extinction.

                     " O poor soul !
When I have thought of such as he, ere now,
It seemed to me the harvest of all woes,
The sum of all the earth's calamities
Was heaped upon them, and that sudden death,

Would be of all things what they most desired
And prayed for most when they invoked their gods ;
And yet this man, this worst of all, this prince
Of all the world's afflicted, as I think,
Betrayed such fear as shewed a love of life
And a keen sense of nice propriety.
And why should they show fear to whom this life
Would seem an awful burthen ? why shun death,
If but a severance from misery
And the deep loathing of their fellow men,
Unless their life has still some pleasant sense
In all its waste of pain and bitterness—
Some green oasis, bright with trees and flowers,
And cool and fresh with never-failing springs
Amidst the weary desert of their ills,
Or some fair island, smiling far away,
In all their ocean of calamity ?
It must be thus ! else had this blighted wretch
Ne'er shown such signs of abject piteous fear.
And I, to think that I inspired such fear !
I, who so oft compassioned such as he,
Myself not granted e'en his poor compassion,
But only feared and fled from.   I so soon
(For it doth seem me as but yesterday)
From being the first woman in the world,
Queen o'er a hundred nations, am proclaimed

The veriest outcast in the universe,
Shunned and avoided most of all that live
Within the shadow of the throne I shared.

" And why ? what have I done against the law ?
What sin have I committed that 's too black
To be forgiven alike of gods and men ?
Have I wrought any mischief in the realm
By covert treason, or unbridled speech ?
Have I been cruel to the populace,
Using th' king's favor to do deeds of blood
Or any manner of oppressive wrong?
Have I strayed from the faith of Zoroaster?
Or failed in aught toward our Persian gods ?
Or kindled the king's wrath against the Magi ?
Or lacked in reverence for Aura Mazda ?
Or of the sacred fire that ever burns
On our hill temples' ever holy altars ?
No, surely no, not any one of these !
Brought I dishonor to the royal bed ?
Or played with my affections for the King ?
Or brought I any scandal to the court ?
Or was I filled with idle vanities
Seeking the praise of all the empire's people,
Save as a woman may at all times seek
The whole world's praise by trying to do good ?

No, no again ! again a thousand times !
How wildly beats my poor heart in my breast
As tho' 't were wounded by the questioned thought !
How does it throb to vindicate itself
Till each pulsation is a clamorous ' No ! '
Have I shown aught but kindness to the King ?
Or, knowing what he willed, have I withheld
To yield unto his will obedience ?
Alas ! my troubled soul doth seem to sink
And almost die within me when I hear
Or think of that one word *obedience.*
For lack of it behold me what I am !
An outcast wanderer, whom to cheer or aid
Is but to court displeasure of the King !
For lack of it I am robbed of a crown
And turned adrift clothed in a beggar's rags .
For lack of it I 've lost a Kingdom's homage,
And found a Kingdom's contumely instead !
For lack of it !—but O my soul ! enough !—
I have lost all I had but this poor life,
And found all I had not, save only death ;
And if I 'd lost or found but one thing more
It had been better ; and the pitying breeze
(All that will listen to my poor complaint)
Had not been burdened with this breath of woe.
And yet 't was only once in all my life,

Then but in form and scarcely so in fact,
That I e'er thought to disobey the King;
For when he sent to me his chamberlains
With the request that I attend at once
Before himself and all the tribute kings
And all the mighty princes of the realm
And the great captains, magnates, and what not,—
To come, crowned, and unveiled before all these ;
I was astonished, grievously perplexed,—
And scarce knew what I did, or what I said,
Or what I ought t' have done ; for I was told
The King was quite hilarious with much wine,
And that the people, and assembled guests,
With mellow vintage all too freely used
Had laid aside much of their dignity,
And in their boist'rous mirth were quaffing still
Even when the King so strangely summoned me
Unto the pillared garden of the feast
To be the target of ten thousand eyes,
All by the King's request turned upon me
To view my beauty.   Over sensative,
I thought of their bold eyes and maudlin speech
(All ten times worse than was the truth, no doubt),—
And it did seem as tho' I could not bear
To undergo an ordeal like that,
And that the King must surely, when he came

To view the matter calmly afterward,
Even praise my action, and himself be glad
I had withheld from coming for a while.
Still did I hesitate, besieged with doubts,
Until I chanced to think that once the King,
After the nuptials, on our wedding day,
Had told me and assured me graciously,
That any wish of mine made known to him,
E'en to the giving of one half his kingdom,
Would speedily be granted. So I thought
This one offence, if such it were construed,
Would straightway be condoned at my request,
(For never had I once besought the King
For any favor, never having need,
For every wish I 'd had ere it found voice
He had anticipated, yea and more),
And thinking so, I bade the chamberlains
To take my poor excuses and regrets,
Which I did frame for them, unto the King,
And if not well received, beg to return
That I might yet go to him ; and they went,
Nor came again, and so for a short time
I thought that all was well ; but soon my soul
Was troubled with misgivings, and next day,
As I sat on a divan 'mong my maids,
My sisters, and the royal company—

To entertain whom in the women's house
Had been for months my pleasant daily duty—
I heard the criers, running thro' the streets,
Proclaiming with loud voice unto the world
Words that at first I could not understand,
But as they came still nearer I did hear :
' *The great King hath decreed, and it is writ*
Down in the chronicles a changeless law
Of Persia, Media, and the Provinces—
Vashti is banned for disobedience
Unto the King, and she shall come no more
Into the presence of the King, forever' ;——

" Darkness !   I heard no more !   I saw no more !
Nor lived I more, for I know not how long ;
For the still silence of unconsciousness
Enwrapt me like a mantle ; till at length,
When the red tide within my rigid veins
Moved once again in its retarded course
(Like day-break struggling thro' a bank of clouds)
And consciousness returned, op'ning my eyes
I saw again the king's seven chamberlains
Standing about me with fixed purposed look,
And all the women pale and horrified
Gazed on me from a little distance back
Wringing their hands and moaning piteously.

My fair dear sisters, too, sobbed in distress,
And my sweet babe, held in his nurse's arms,
Stretched forth his little hands and crooned to me ;
Then for a moment all again was dark.
But, rallying, I tried to catch my thoughts
When one of the sev'n spake and said to me
(His voice as steady as a wall of stone
His heart as seeming cold and pitiless) :
' We 're come to tell thee of the king's decree,
In part, in part to put it into force.'

" Then he related that which I had heard
And this still further of the written law :
' *That her estate be given to another*
Better than she, her raiment, and her crown,
Her jewels, and her gold—all that she hath
Is forfeited ; and in coarse convict garb
She shall be turned without the palace gates
To come no more within them. In the streets
All unattended shall she be put forth
To go whereso she listeth——'

" ' 'T is enough ! '
I cried, ' enough ! Oh, let me hear no more !
Go thou, Mehuman ! for thy heart is kind,
Oh, go ! and but implore the King for me

That he give me a moment's audience—
That he stretch forth the golden sceptre now
And let me on my bended knees approach
To plead my poor cause with his Majesty
And free my soul from this imputed wrong !
Oh, go ! and but remind him of his vow
(Made on the day that he made me his queen)
That any wish of mine should be his law
Unto its proper granting ; and that now
I humbly crave expression for my wish
In his imperial presence, for the sake
Of our sweet son, our pretty baby prince.
Frame this in thy own words, I know thou canst ! '

" Poor soul ! kind-hearted, fearless Mehuman !
Even as I spake the muscles of his face
Twitched with emotion, and his well-knit frame
Was all a-tremble, for, so, my deep grief
Had touched with sympathy his ev'ry nerve ;
And tho' *he* knew, not *I*, I 'd asked so much,
Consigning him to a worse fate than mine,
I saw his lips compress like plates of iron
Impinging each on each ; even as he turned
And vowed to do my bidding, while the rest
Stood coldly, unconcernedly anear,
As tho' 't were matter of small consequence

However my poor pray'r should be received,
Or what reply my messenger should bring ;
But now I blame them not : too well they knew
The hopelessness of my forlorn appeal
From what in Persia hath been once decreed,
And that 't was dangerous to show concern
In such a matter.
                           " Soon Mehuman came
Returning from the presence of the King
And as he did approach I soon observed
A deathly pallor was upon his face ;
And then I knew full well there was no hope ;
Yet that brave tongue that dared to plead for me
Spake once again, because I did command—
Spake then, and thus, then spake again no more :
' *The King denies thy suit, retorting that*
The promise which he made was to the queen
And that thou art not such ; and that the King
More than the subject may not break the law,—
Bade me return to execute the law
And drave me forth in anger.'

                                   " Why I lived,
Or how I could live, after hearing this
I know not, but the first wild surging flood
Of anguish that had swept across my soul

Had left me little more that I could suffer ;
And these strange, awful words but stupefied
The keenness of my grief and left me mute,
Brooding upon my great calamity
Until cold Carcas, foremost of the seven,
Came near to me and took from off my head
The jewelled diadem of Persia's queen ;
And the rare necklace of white shimmering pearls
He loosened from their place, and one by one
Bade me take off my bracelets and my rings,
The coil of diamonds plaited in my hair,
And all the jewels that adorned my robes ;
Then called two female slaves to lead me forth
Into a chamber to disrobe me there
And clothe me for expulsion to the streets.

"Soon it was done, and I led out again
A convict outcast, like a menial clad,
To look my last farewell with frenzied eyes
At the fair court where I had reigned a queen—
At my sweet home of beauty, mine no more ;
But all things else seemed trivial and vain,
In that sad moment of supreme despair,
To parting with my child, my pretty boy,
Whom they were plucking from his mother's breast—
Whom they were tearing from my bleeding heart ;

And when I begged to see him once again,
To kiss his rosebud lips, and clasp his form,
And feel the pressure of his velvet cheek,
They brought him to me ; it was good of them,—
An act of kindness that it seemed to me
Was worth to me more than the world beside,
As his fair dimpled arms twined round my neck
And his pure infant heart beat its light rhythm
Against the heavy pulsings of my own,
And the sweet innocent mouth to my parched lips
Pressed   showers   of   kisses,   and   cooed,   ' Mamma,'
    ' Mamma,'
Rousing my spirit so surcharged with grief,
With such a subtle thrill of ecstasy
That it did seem the conflict of the two
Would end in madness.

                " Then thus Carcas spake :
' It is enough !   We must perform our duty !
Now put away the child, and get thee hence ! '
And laying hands on me they held me fast
Forcing my little one from my embrace,
And bearing him away from me, mid sobs
Of my affrighted sisters ; then again
The darkness came upon me, and without
They carried me at will and left me there
5

A worse than beggar, lying on the street,
Upon the border-land 'twixt life and death.

" The sad awakening!   Oh, speech fails my lips
To give expression to the wretchedness—
The deep humiliating sense, the woe,
That crept upon me with returning life.
I tried to reason with, and know, myself,
For I did seem a puzzle to myself.
To see myself in such a wretched garb—
To find myself abandoned and ignored—
To know that even then a thousand men,
Urged on a thousand horses at their speed
From Shushan, trav'ling, like diverging rays
Out from a central sun, to reach at length
The farthest limit of the mighty realm,
And that each bore with him a formal script,
Bearing the King's sign-manual and seal,
To every ruler in the Provinces,
Writ in the sev'ral various tongues of each,
Proclaiming my dishonor by the law,
And ordering these again to publish it
To all their people, so that my disgrace
And degradation might be known to all—
To see, to feel, to know all this and live,
To live and still not be a maniac,

Was something that I can but marvel at.
How am I fallen from mine high estate !
How am I punished for a thoughtless word
Spoken in kindness and with good intent !—
And punished, too, for what was not forbidden.

" Somewhere, I 've heard, that 'mong the Israelites
'T is held their God created the first pair
And placed them on this earth in happiness,
Woman and man, their ev'ry want supplied ;
Without a care or task to make them tired,
Without a sorrow or a twinge of pain,
Without the knowledge or the fear of death
Nor under death's domain, being immortal ;
That in a wondrous garden where they dwelt
Were trees of beauty whose wide-spreading boughs
Thatched with their own bright leaves, forever green,
Sheltered their bodies from the mid-day sun,
And formed the circling bow'rs 'neath which they
        passed
Their honeyed hours of sleep and mutual love ;
That over them the sky forever blue
Smiled in calm majesty, and bloomed at night
With all its countless myriads of stars
Always unclouded ; that a river flowed
Broad and meandering thro' their fair domain,

Which lay beyond the Tigris, and its clear
And peaceful waters, and the dews of night
Sustained all life without the fall of rain.
The brightest flowers were in perpetual bloom,
The air forever laden with sweet scents,
The fairest birds sang sweetest liquid notes
Within the groves, and ev'ry living thing
That moved upon the earth, or in the air,
Was round about them 'biding all in peace,
And over all, and all things that had life
And moved within the waters, had they charge
And full dominion ; and of all the trees,
Bearing much fruit of many divers kinds,
None was denied them save the fruit of one
That stood out plainly in the garden's midst
And hung with clusters tempting to the eye—
Forbidden fruit, which they were warned against
And told that but to taste of it were death ;
And, that, being tempted much, by Ahriman
(The Evil Spirit, in a serpent's form)—
Telling her that to eat of that one tree
The fruit their God had thus denied to them
Would be to make them as the gods in wisdom
And in all knowledge,—the duped woman ate,
And having eaten bade her husband eat,
And he, out of compassion for his wife,

Willed that to suffer with her for her wrong
Was but his duty, and could scarce be worse
Than to be robbed of her sweet company,
And so he ate, and having eaten, both
Were driven from the garden in deep shame,
No more immortal, but consigned to death
With all their offspring, down thro' all the ages,
Thenceforth to eat the bread of bitterness
Wrung by their toil from the unwilling earth !

" Oh, that was heavy punishment indeed !
Yet was it but the penalty laid down
As price of disobedience.   But with me
The prohibition and the penalty—
That which forbids and that which punishes
The thing for which I suffer—had no life
Till after the commission of the act
Which it declared a crime and visited
In the same day with the dire penalties
Which now are crushing me without appeal—
Without a single word in my behalf
Being uttered or allowed.

                              " Can this be just ?
No ! gods and men alike proclaim it.   No !
Yet I blame not the King, but Memucan

Whose vengeful spirit sought my overthrow
For some deep, hidden purpose of his own ;
For when he found the King in angered mood
Before the 'semblage making inquiry
What should be done to me ; he spake no word
Extenuating in the least my fault,
Nor held himself content to name my sentence
Till he had first aroused the king's hot wrath
Still further 'gainst me by his poisoned words
To the sustaining of the thing he sought,
Charging my wrong as 'gainst both King and princes,
Aye, and against all people of the land,
And prophesying that my wayward act
Would soon unseat all husbands from their pow'r
If unrebuked ; then named my punishment,
That, when decreed, all wives might thenceforth honor
Their husbands duly, and obey them well.

" And has it come that men, in their proud strength
And boasted courage, need to be sustained,
And their authority decreed, by law,
Over their wives ?   Fie on his sophistry !
Fie on the weakling princes who could stand
And thus be parties to their own dishonor,
By speaking not against the thing proposed,
Belittling all manhood, crushing me.

But what have I to do now with resentment,
Or anything but sorrow ?

" Lo ! now come
People with skins and vessels to the pool
To get supply of water for the day !
Have I delayed so long? an hour or more,
Discoursing of myself unto myself?
And yet when none else hear I needs must talk,—
Not being free to talk at other times,—
It doth divide my grief to bring my wrongs
To mine own hearing in the form of speech,
And call to feeling's aid another sense
To share the load it scarce can bear alone.
Now must I be away ! the day is long,
But still the night will come, and when it doth,
Beneath its friendly darkness I may find
Some sheltering nook where I may hide myself
And seek the dearest boon that 's left me,—sleep."

BOOK III.

SO Persia was made queenless ! but 't is writ
That all the fairest maidens of the realm
Were called to Shushan—summoned 'fore the King,
As it had been appointed by his Court,
So she who most might please the King should be
Made queen in Vashti's stead.   Some time ere this,
Within her humble home, fair Hadassah,
Jew Mordecai's cousin and his ward—
A daughter of the Tribe of Benjamin
Whose father's father, once again removed,
Had with King Jeconiah been driven forth
To Babylon with the Captivity,—
Standing one day before her crafty kinsman
Noted his gaze fixed most intently on her,
And his lips parted, as tho' he would speak,
Yet spake not ; so she spake unto him, saying :

" My more than father, speak ! What is thy thought ?
What dost thou see in me to fix thine eyes
So searchingly upon me ? "   And the Jew,
As if awakening from a reverie,
Drew his right hand across his brow and said :
" My child, my Hadas', thou art very fair ;
Thy form is straight and supple, and thy face
Hath that about it, that, once looked upon,
Makes the beholder long to look again,
To study, it may be, what subtle something
Maketh its rare attraction.   Even so,
I, who have raised thee, child, and know thee well
Most from thy infancy, have felt this truth,
Yet ne'er before so strongly as but now,
When thou didst speak to me.   Before, it seemed
As doth the dawn stealing upon the earth,
Faintly, at first, but with increasing light
Dissolving in itself the ling'ring shadows ;
But now 't is as the mid-day's harvest glory
In ripe fruition.   Not thy shapely neck
Bearing so gracefully thy queenly head ;
Not thy well-rounded chin and blooming cheeks ;
Not thy arched nose with its proud curving nostrils ;
Not thy dark mournful eyes that look from 'neath
The arches which support thy lofty brow
With such a light of truth and tenderness ;

Not thy black silken locks,—thy present crown;—
Not any one of these have moved me thus,
Nor all together ; tho' these were enough,
Within themselves, to move all others so.
But I see in thy face the trust of Hagar,
The kindness of Rebecca at the well,
The faith of Miriam, the love of Ruth,
Rispah's devotion, and Naomi's care,
Each having for its object, Israel—
Israel oppressed, down-trodden, and despised
(Bearing the railings of vindictive men),
Israel dispersed, and stripped of temp'ral pow'r
(Bearing the judgments of an angered God).
O daughter mine ! I see in thee the glory
Of all the womanhood of all our race
Linked with our manhood's hope for Israel !—
Nay, think me not a flatterer, or crazed,
But hearken further :

          " In a fortnight's time
Will the king's couriers override the land
To gather to the palace of the king
The fairest of the maidens of the empire
To go before the King, as 't is decreed ;
So that the one who best shall please the King
Shall be his queen, the queen of all this realm,

Even as Vashti was that is deposed :
Now I believe me that in all the realm
There 's not a fairer maiden than art thou,
But thou 'rt a Jewess, and if this were known
'T would bar thee from this contest for a crown
As if thou wert an outcast. Yet my soul
Hath a fixed, purposed faith, and sure belief,
That queen thou mayest be, if queen thou wilt,
So hear with patience :

            " Thou art little known
Outside this village, thou hast never been
About the palace since I at the court
Have been one of the keepers at the gate,—
Nor ever been at Shushan, unless veiled
After the custom that these shamefaced Gentiles
Have taught their women. Now, our long-time friend
Rohaman-Ismail, the apostate Jew,
Hath grown rich in the land, and prospered well.
He hath two daughters, younger each than thou,
And but the other day did send me word
To let thee come to them at Ecbatana—
Whither they now do dwell—and bide with them
Awhile, for thy own pleasure and their good,
The while he doth intend to Araby
To make a venture with his caravan

With various merchandise promising profit,
And it would please me well if thou wouldst go.

" Mount our best dromedary, take our Hamish—
A servant ever faithful and discreet—
Close veil thy face, if any be near by,
Take thy best wardrobe with thee, and thy lute,
And journey forthwith to Ecbatana
Starting upon the morrow ; and when there,
Stay at our friend's as he invited thee.
At no time make it known that thou 'rt a Jewess
(Thou may'st be sure our friends will never do so),
But do thou as our friends do,—mention not
Thy home or kindred ; wear thy best attire
And—as thou always dost—a winning smile ;
Be merry, use thy lute and thy sweet voice
As best thou mayest. Further, as their guest,
Seem gracious, yet not humble, to our friends,
And to their friends, whom thou may'st chance to meet.

Sing, rather than converse, to entertain,
For speech hath e'er more tell-tale lips than song.
Observe these things and ere three moons shall pass
Thou shalt be summoned to the palace Shushan
A candidate for Persia's queenly crown :
Wilt go as I would have thee ? "

Hadassah,
Regarding Mordecai with surprise
Mingled with doubt and fear, answered him thus :
" My kinsman and my father, save in name,
Thy wish, as thy command hath been till now
And so still must be, if thy truthful wish,
My guide in action ; yet doth thy strange words
Seem like the small enkindling of a flame
That may consume us both.   Never before
Have I heard flattery escape thy lips
To *any* person, and much less to me
Whom thou hast warned against all flattering speech
As 'gainst contagion.   Always, until now,
Hast thou advised me 'gainst the sinful folly
Thou called'st ' the world's ambition and the pride
Of earthly riches, and the lust of pow'r ' ;
Always till now hast thou instructed me
To shun these heathen Persians and these Medes
Whom it hath been our fate to dwell amongst ;
While an apostate from the Jewish faith
Hath seemed the special horror of thy soul ;
And now, what sayest thou ?   Thy ardent words
Spoken in praise of what thou callest my beauty,
Had, from another's lips, earned thy rebuke
As idle folly.   In my maiden ear
Thou pourest now the dulcet, burning music

Of an ambition wilder than the dreams
Of youth's enchanted slumbers.   Whom I've shunned,
As thou hast wished—and I was pleased to shun—
Thou now wouldst have me seek, and in disguise
Unworthily scheme to be one of them—
One of the very chiefest of them all ;
And by so doing to disown myself,
Deny my people and deny my God,
Earn for myself the curse of Israel,
And failing (as I doubt not I should fail),
The scoffs and jeers of these unholy Gentiles,
My own reproach, thy unavailing pity,
And the world's instance of aspiring folly
Justly rebuked.

               " Is 't truly then thy wish
That I shall dwell in an apostate's house
(Albeit I know this one hath that about him
Which doth hold captive thy reluctant friendship),
And from this vantage-ground, with base deceit
Practise the pretty wiles of which thou speakest
That I might thus attract the dull attention
Of the king's pandering slaves, and so be chosen,
Not as the chance might fall, but, through intrigue?—
My own intrigue, and thy intrigue ; for what?
For the one chance—a chance among the thousands,

To air my charms before this haughty King—
To surely play the harlot, with the hope,
Thereby to win approval and a crown,
And lose my self-respect scarcely the less
Whether I win a crown or lose mine honor ;
To win a husband, should I win at all,
Who is too great and terrible to love—
Too powerful and rash to reason with,
And therefore would exact the toll of love,
Lip service and a reverential mien,
Even where love was not ; and his anger roused
My life might scarce assuage it, and my fate
Be even sadder than the banished Vashti's.
What say'st thou ? is 't thy wish that I shall go ? "

Then Mordecai thus :
               " Cousin, thy words
Are searching as the thrust of warrior's spear,
And keen as wintry winds to the unclad.
That they have weight, as well as worldly wisdom,
I 'll not dispute. That thou hast strength and courage
To hold to light my seeming inconsistence,
Argues thee well, and calls for no rebuke.
Thy gentle spirit, that I ne'er before
Have seen moved to such depths of eloquence,
Shews a new charm of undiscovered power,

Which, conscious of itself, in sweet reluctance
Offers to sacrifice its own convictions
And do my wish in strict obedience
E'en to self-seeming ruin :   This the more
Doth fix the deep conviction of my soul,
That queen thou oughtest be, and so thou must ;
For as my soul doth live, but yesternight
I dreamed of thee (and I do seldom dream).
I dreamed that all the court and palace Shushan
Was gay with banners and illumed with lamps ;
That a great throng was gathered in the court
And in the midst of them, in shining robes,
Upon a golden throne, beside the king's,
Raised on a marble dais, thou wert seated,
When lo, the King himself, even Ahasuerus,
Stepped close beside thee bearing in his hands
A triple golden zone, studded with gems,
Which he himself did place upon thy head
And called the throng to view thy coronation
And give it witness.   Then in loud acclaim
Tumultuous, the raptured throng burst forth
Till the court seemed to quiver with the power
Of their glad-voiced hosannahs ; and the King,
Taking thee by the hand, bade thee arise,
And there proclaimed thee Queen, and named thee
     ' Esther.'

And when I heard the name I cried aloud
Unto the God of glory,—as it seemed :
' This surely is the token ! this the star
Risen once more to beacon Judah on
In light and safety ! '

"Hadas' ! cousin !
My vision is upon me like a spell,
And will not be ignored or put aside,
But in mine ears that multitudinous voice
Is ringing still with shouts of ' Long live Esther ! '
' Esther the beautiful ; our honored queen ! '
' Fair Star of Persia, live, live on forever ! '
And in all this I find a hope for Jewry,
For wert thou but the queen, our smitten race
Had then a faithful friend near to the throne
Whose sweet persuasion and discerning wit
Might stand between us and the machinations
Of our fierce enemies, who in their hate
Should seek the sanction of the hasty King
To our undoing. I have weighed thy scruples,
And in the scale of ordinary things
Naught can be placed to keep the beam in poise ;
But that I hope, is not for thee alone,
And surely not for me, but for our people—
Not for our glory, but for Israel's good
6

And for the glory of the great Jehovah.
Thy scruples are of evil, but the soul
Which looks beyond the act to the result,
And that result be the great good of many,
Whereas, the act effects that soul alone—
And be not gloried in, or undertaken
Save for the good that is to come of it,
Where is the evil ?   Surely there is none !
For so, the act, the soul reluctantly
Weaves in the master purpose, which is good.
Further, my Hadas', this thing only, further :
In this great opportunity I see
The hand of the Almighty stretching forth
To touch, once more, the wounds of Israel
With healing pity."

                    " Cousin, 't is enough !
I will not question more ! "   Hadassah cried,
" Forgive thou my presumption and my doubts,
For surely now I know this is thy wish,
And that alone, for me, were all-sufficient,
But if it be God's will, as thou believest,
It would be impious to hesitate,
And so I will set forth at early morn
For Ecbatana, even as thou sayest
To do and act in all things."

" 'T is well said.
My child, my faithful Hadas', " cried the Jew ;
" And may God speed the coming of thy glory,
Than which, as I beheld it in my dream,
None shall be greater throughout all the earth
Among all women."

Long before the dawn,
While yet the stars shone from a moonless sky
Upon the silent, fertile Susian plains,
Pursuing for a time their northward course
Along the western bank of the Chaospes,
O'er the brown, dusty, trampled thoroughfare,
Hadassah and the grave, gray-bearded Hamish,
Each mounted on a tall, swift-footed camel,
Rode thoughtfully along.   Another beast,
That bore light camp equipage and provision,
Followed behind, led by a leathern thong
Which the old servant held within his hand
Or fastened to his girdle.   Thus began
That wondrous journey to Ecbatana,
Whose whole effect not Mordecai dreamed
Or mortal man conjectured.   Little spake,
These early trav'llers in the star-lit silence,
For all about them seemed so filled with awe
So wrapt in the still majesty of night,

That speech fell on their ears like the intrusion
Of jarring sounds, in that vast harmony
Of overarching sky and sleeping plain
And low-breathed murmurs of a dreaming world.

At length the first signs of approaching day
Crept up the eastern sky, and grew in strength,
Until the bright rays of the coming sun
Ribbed half the heavens with light.   Then there ap-
      peared
Close to a little thicket by the way,
A lion, crouching as if he would spring
Upon the maiden and her gray-beard escort,
Yet sprang not ; but arising to his height
With flaming eyes looked in Hadassah's face,
And, lashing, with his tail, his tawny sides,
Ope'd his fanged jaws and from his ruddy throat
Poured a triumphant roar that set the air
A-tremble o'er the plain ; then turning fled
Even to'ard Shushan.   Hamish, white with fear,
Spake not, altho' his lips essayed to speak,
And their affrighted beasts at ev'ry joint
Quaked in dumb terror.   Hadassah,
For some strange cause she could not understand,
Felt naught of trepidation or alarm,
But, turning in her houdah, watched the lion

Leaping in rapid flight, and then she saw
The distant peaks aflame with filmy gold,
And then the sunshine from those glowing summits
Slipt down to eastward on the arid plain
Sweeping toward them, till great Shushan's towers—
Now left behind—were bathed in its warm lustre.
Then turning unto Hamish, Hadas' spake :

" Be not afraid ! The lion has gone hence !
'T was strange that he should lie in wait for us
And thus confront us with his savage presence,
Pour out the thunders of his awful voice,
Yet flee and harm us not. 'T was also strange
He should be here at all. No lion else,
As I believe, hath been for many years
North far as Shushan. As my soul doth live,
And as my eyes behold this wondrous morn—
The fairest that I ever looked upon,—
There is a potent augury in this
That bodes us well ; for out of Egypt came,
Before the Bondage, and from Israel's lips,
As on his couch he sate delaying death
To speak his parting charge unto his sons—
His dying blessing and his prophecy—
Words full of hope for Judah. Lo, he fixed,
As thou rememb'rest to have seen it writ,

A couchant lion as our tribal emblem,
And asketh—' Who shall rouse him ? ' "

　　　　　　　　　　　　" O, my God !
Hath this, then, portent of deliverance ?
Have I aroused the Lion of our Tribe
Thus in the semblance of a savage beast
Unto my people's betterment, or safety ?
So may it prove !　At least I go content
On this strange journey I am set upon
With hope aroused and with a pray'rful heart,
Fearing no evil."

　　　　　　　　So they journeyed on
These two, for the most part in speechless silence
Plodding day after day the weary road,
Halting at eve to feed their tired beasts
And to refresh themselves ; the evening meal
Prepared there by the wayside, and partaken,
The faithful Hamish pitched the tiny tent,
And, when the maid withdrew therein and slept,
Lay down without the door, wrapt in his robes,
To guard his mistress, gaze up at the stars,
And the dim, silent summits of the Zagros,
And muse on the strange fortunes of his race,
Till weariness and safety bade him sleep.

And so day followed day, and oft they met
Upon the way some Median caravan
Bearing rich stores of grain, and spicery,
Peltries, and products of the Median looms,
Down to the great King's capitol for sale.
The drivers and the merchants looked surprised
At the veiled maiden and her aged attendant.
But these delayed not, nor asked any question,
Nor were they questioned. Surely these they passed
Knew not that Persia's queen, so soon to be,
Had ridden by them. After twenty days
The travellers had reached the grassy flank
Of Mount Orontes, and the battlements
Of Ecbatana's tower came into view,
And soon the whole great city was around them,
With its strange sights, its many cooling fountains,
And rich, luxuriant gardens all abloom
With roses of a hundred various tints
Shedding sweet perfumes. Mordecai's friends
Received the maiden joyfully among them,
Whence she was soon sought out for her great beauty
And taken down to Shushan, where in time,
Even as Mordecai saw it in his dream,
She was made queen ; and all the court was wild
With much rejoicing ; and the feast was spread ;
Queen Esther's name was upon ev'ry lip ;

And all the empire echoed with the praise
Of her great charms ; for surely she was fair,
And she was queen ; the King's own fav'rite star ;
And no one spake of Vashti any more,
For Vashti was as one long dead, to those
Who fawned upon the King. But the new queen
Disclosed not yet her race, and few indeed
Surmised that Israel shared Iran's throne.

BOOK IV.

B IGTHAN, and Teresh—brethren of Mehuman
Whose sight had been destroyed and whose tongue
    silenced
By the command of the revengeful King
For daring to present Vashti's appeal—
In pond'ring on their kinsman's deadly wrongs
Conspired to slay the King, and thus avenge
Their brother's cruel maims ; and noting not
The seeming listless Jew who sate betimes
In the King's gate outside the door they guarded,
They dropt, now and again, a word whose meaning
Was thought to be unreadable, except
By application of the awful key
Possessed by them alone. But as he sate
With gaze intent upon the marble pave,
The keen wits of the Jew were gath'ring up
A stray word here, a broken sentence there,
And fitting these together in his mind,

Supplying now a thought, and then a query
Connected with the gossip of the court
And his own knowledge of some past events,
Their daring plot was opened to his view,
And he did presently divulge the same.
Seizure and sentence followed ; and the twain,
Seeking revenge for a brave brother's wrongs,
Found only for themselves death on the gallows.
Then was it entered in the chronicles
How Mordecai had preserved the empire,
In that he had preserved the mighty King,
Its front and centre. But the matter passed ;
And Haman, a designing Agagite,
A long time in great favor with the King,
Press'd for still further favor and more pow'r,
And not in vain, till, save the King himself,
Not any was above him. When he passed
Heads were uncovered, and the suppliant knee
Bended at his approach. All did him honor ;
All save one—the Jew,—and he ignored
Not only the pretensions, but the presence
Of the exalted one ; who in his turn
Conceived so fierce a hatred of the Jew
That his extinction could not well appease,
And the annihilation of his race
Throughout the realm, alone might satisfy.

So Haman sought the King, and craftily
Charged Jewry with a lack of loyalty,
Dis'bedience to the laws, and covert treason ;
And as a measure for the King's own safety,
And the well-being of the mighty realm,
Urged ev'ry Hebrew's death ; off'ring himself
To pay much money in the treasury
To prove his zeal was for the nation's good
And not for his own ends.   The King, alarmed,
And acting rashly, as it was his wont,
Persuaded by the favorite's calumnies
So cunningly paraded as the truth,
Granted the tenor of his cruel prayer
And caused it to be written in the law
As verity, and made unchangeable,
And gave his ring to seal it, and the doom
Of Israel ; for therein 't was decreed :

" That, on the thirteenth day of the month Adar,
   The power of this realm, hereby invoked,
   Shall, throughout all our many provinces,
   By all our satraps and our tribute kings
   (Who, for the perfect carrying out whereof   ·
   As herein made of record and decreed,
   Are held to strict accountability)
   Directing the armed forces of our realm,

And all the populace available,
Within their sev'ral satrapies and states,
Visit sure death upon the hated Jews,
Pernicious in themselves, and full of menace
To the realm's safety. Women, children, men,
Aged and young alike, let none be spared ;
So that our realm be safely rid of them
Then and forever ; and, moreover, this :
That of all Hebrews slain their goods shall be
A prey to their destroyers."

                                   This, so writ
Was formally attested, duly sealed,
And ordered published throughout all the realm,
After the manner of all Persian laws,
In all the provinces, to all the rulers
To be proclaimed by them to all the people ;
And Mordecai, when he heard of it,
Was bowed with grief, and clamorous with despair,
And, rending all his garments, then threw dust
Upon his head, and went about the streets
Troubling the day and night with bitter wail
And lamentation.
                    " O Jerusalem ! "
He cried, " rearing thy glorious head once more
From thine own ruins, now may'st thou behold

The more than ruin of thy smitten people,—
Their legalized destruction ! Let thy walls,
Thy holy temple, and thy goodly towers,
So lately resurrected, sink again,
And seek oblivion in the dust of earth
That soon shall hide the last of all thy builders !
Thus may our race, and thou, our well-beloved,
Perish together ! Woe, O Israel,
Woe is thy portion ! The Egyptian's yoke,
The wanderers' sufferings in the wilderness,
Assyria's cruel tasks, Babylon's gibes
Through generations of captivity,
Have stained with grief the pages of thy script,
And now this Persian terror seals the book
And binds the volume of thy sorrows all
In death's completion ! Weep, ye Jewish maids !
And mourn, as Jephtha's daughter wept and mourned,
For the warm love that leaps in all your veins
Must die ungathered, even as did hers,
And that without availment ! Cry ye out,
Mothers of Israel, for your babes must die,
First-born and last ! but this last Pharaoh
Decrees that ye die with them, so your grief
Shall not be of long life ! Lo, Judah, now,
Behold the open graves digged for thy people
And them be dumb forever ! Is this all ?

Why did I hope for Israel any more ?
O God, why did I dream those wondrous dreams
That have been honored like true prophecy
In their fulfilment, and then live to see,
This day, the crumbling down in bitterness
Of more than all I hoped for ! "

                                    As he called
His lamentations thus, pacing the pave
Before the palace gate, tattered and grimed,
The eunuch Hatach, bearing in his hands
A parcel, came and spake unto him thus :
" Sir, the queen hath heard of thy condition
And of thy bitter wailings, and the knowledge
That thou didst on a time befriend the King
Moved her compassion, and so she hath sent
This raiment for thee, that thou may'st be clad
As doth befit thee ; and she further 'quireth
The cause of thy lamenting.   Don this garb,
And then relate to me thy heavy sorrow
That I may speak it to her, and mayhap
She can befriend thee in such way as shall
In measure stay thy grief."

                          Then Hatach held
Toward the Jew the raiment he had brought,
But Mordecai put it from him, saying :

" Take it away ! What need have I of raiment
Except to rend it ? Why should I be clothed
Except in sackcloth ? 'Naked to the world,'
As Job cried out of old, 'I came !' And now,
I and my people must, by law, be stript,
And given o'er to death in nakedness;
For which a price is paid in privilege !
These, sorrow's tatters, that now cling to me,
Indifferently serve to hide my shame,—
That is enough ! And if the queen would know
Why I do mourn, then bear thou this to her ! "
Saying which the Jew handed the wond'ring Hatach
A written scroll and copy of the law
So late decreed against the Jews, and added :
" Tell her to read it and consider well
If I have cause for sorrow ! Further,
Tell her the time is come that she must act !
She must declare herself, and sue the King
For mercy to our people ! "

                              Wond'ring that
The Jew should hazard such a speech as this
For message to the queen, Hatach returned
And gave the queen the scroll and verbal message,
Which when she had perused and listened to,
She seemed amazed and troubled beyond measure.

The color fled her cheeks, leaving her face
White as the alabaster statue, by her side,
Of a winged griffin, which she caught upon
To save herself from falling.   Then she turned
As if to hide her face from the dazed eunuch
Until her young heart drove the truant blood
Back to its place with fluttering little throbs.
But she exclaimed not, tho' it seemed to her
As if the hopes which she had builded up
Lay at her feet in ruins, and the fears
And doubts she first had felt arose again
In the deep shadow of this pending doom
That threatened Israel.   Yet she stilled her dread
And tried to think what word she must return
Back to the Jew, for tho' no hope appeared
In Mordecai's hint as to her duty,
She did not wholly yield up to despair.
Still, knowing not what else to say to him,
And seeing the immediate demand
For answer in some sort unto the Jew,
She spake to Hatach thus :

                    " Tell thou the Jew
That I compassion with him and his people,
And fain would do some act to succor them,
Yet know the law is such, that to approach

The august presence of the mighty King
Within the inner court where he is found,
Unless so bidden by the King himself,
Whether 't be woman or man that venture it,
Death is the forfeit, save, indeed, to such
As it may please the King that he extend
To'ard them the golden sceptre, saying ' Live ! '
These thirty days hath not the King beheld
My face or sent to bid me come to him !
What might I then expect, to go unbidden
Into his presence, and on such an errand ? "

And so did Hatach speak those, the queen's words,
As bidden, to the Jew, who this returned
In answer unto Esther :   " Now thou 'rt queen
Wilt thou prove false and recreant to thy race
In this the hour of their supremest peril ?
Think not to 'scape with life in the King's house,
If Israel die, more than the meanest slave
Whose veins course with the blood of Abraham !
And if deliverance come, as may God grant,
And thou makest no attempt to forward it,
Destruction then may seize thy father's house,
And on anothers' head the crown of glory
Rest, that I fain would think is only thine ;
And, as I must believe, thou hast been sent

7

To be a queen for such a strait as this,
Let not the time escape thee !   Dost thou fear ?
Surely thou hast great cause !   but will 't be lessened
By waiting death that must engulf us all,
Making no effort, quietly submitting
To perish with the Jewish multitude
And fill a nameless grave ?   No ! rather dare
To die, if die thou must, pleading for life
For all of Israel ; then were thy life
An offering on the altar of thy race,
And so thy death (which may our God forbid !)
A spectacle to move th' offended world,
Making thy name and fame less sacred only
Than if thou shalt succeed in this great cause,
And save thy suff'ring people and thyself
To the Almighty's glory ! "

                              Hatach, so
Told Mordecai's message to the queen
Which when she 'd heard, she sent thro' him again
This writing to the Jew :   " I am resolved !
Gather our people up throughout the city,
And bid them all for me, and in my name,
Give quittance from all toil, and mourn with me,
And fast, and pray, for three full days and nights,
Eating, or drinking, not ; and thinking only

Of our great peril and Jehovah's power :
The same will also I, and all my maids,
And when this time is done, I will proceed
Unbidden to the King, which is unlawful,
And, if I lose my life, then be it so ;
If not I have my plans to intercede
For Israel, according as I may."

So did Jew Mordecai, with his people,
As bidden by the queen ; and Israel mourned,
And mourning wept, and weeping cried aloud,
And wailed her songs of sorrow to the winds,
And rent her garments, took no food or drink,
But dwelt in desolation, praying much
And fearing greatly, for the world was dark.

BOOK V.

LITTLE META.

" COME hither, little maid, and sit thee here
On this poor mat beside me, whiles I try
To tell the thing which thou inquirest of
According to the truth. 'Say whom thou art?'
Poor child ! There was a time when these four words
In thy plain query, now so simply put,
Had found me readier to answer them,
Or, if I hesitated, it had been
For other reasons than oppress me now ;
And yet it is a thing that oftentimes
In these near half-score years I 've asked myself,
And have not found the words to answer me—
From lack of knowledge or from fear of truth—
As seems unto me right.
                    " But this I am,—
A homeless creature, even like thyself,
And one who loves thee dearly, little maid,

And **owes** thee much, and prizes thee yet more,
As the one object that my hungry heart
Hath left to feed its famished love upon
Beholding with mine eyes.
                    " Blessed be the day
I found thee shivering at the evening's close
Upon the wind-swept street, and heard thy sobs
Breaking convulsively, as thou didst call
' Mother ! O mother ! ' ever and anon,
Whilst weakly tugging at the prostrate form
Of her whose name thou spake, who answered not ;
For death had called her ; and I being veiled—
And knowing only of thy great distress—
And being so unknown to those who came
To carry off thy dead, persuaded thee
To come away with me ; for well I knew
That friendlessness and poverty were thine,
And being peers in these, I 'd harm thee not
By offering my love ; tho, when so doing,
I felt I should be doubly well repaid
Even in the like I should receive from thee,
And it hath been so.
                    " So I am thy friend,
And this poor hovel that doth shelter us,
This is our home—a sorry home at best
And yet 't is only ours by sufferance.

" Three years agone, while shivering with cold
And pinched with hunger, I intruded here,
Finding this shelter vacant, and apart
From where much people frequent or pass by
And in the Hebrew quarter of the town
Where Medes or Persians dwell not ; so I came,
And none has spoken to, or questioned me
Of my possession ; nor, until thou camest,
Did any soul look in on me, to know
Whether I lived or died ; but oft I found,
Placed near the door without, small store of food
Left in the moonless night, by whom, I know not,
But I surmise, by some kind-hearted Jew
Who thought me poor and needy, not amiss,
Yet dared not do a deed of charity,
To such as he suspected me to be,
Save under cover of the silent night
When none might see it.
                        "So is charity
Afraid before my face to show herself,
But now, thanks be to thee, my little friend,
These pretty trinkets, that my hands hath learned
To fashion from the grasses, palms, and flowers,
Hath found a market, through thy diligence,
Among the rich where thou dost carry them
To sell and buy us bread.

"I am thy charge,
Thou seest, little maid, well as thy friend,
And one who seeks the place within thy heart,
Of the lost mother I have told thee of
Who cannot come to thee."

"O, my mistress !
Mother thou art, and hast been, unto me,
In many, many ways ! " the child replied,
" For thou dost love me, yes, I know it well,
And thou hast been so very kind to me,
Speaking so sweetly aye, and aye so gently,
So like the singing of the nightingale
For pitying tenderness ; and thou 'rt so good,
And thou 'rt so very fair, so different
In all things from all people I have known
That I do often wonder— It seems strange
That thou shouldst care for a poor beggar's child
Found friendless in the streets : for, O my mistress !
Thou wert not always poor and in distress !
Thy sweetness must have grown among the flowers,
Thy voice developed 'mong the songs of birds
And thy kind heart fed long on tenderness
Hedging thee all around ; and so, forgive me !
Before I thought, the words that were within me
Leaped to my lips which oped to utter them
In the unseemly question I have asked——"

" Hark ! what is that ! "
      ' T was Vashti who exclaimed ;
And both were mute ; and listening, they heard
The deep, slow-measured voice, wondrous in power,
And richness, and unutterable pathos,
Of one who seemed to speak 'mid a great throng
Voicing the prayer of the multitude
Which crouched, or knelt about him with fixed eyes
Centred upon him, as he stood among them,
Each hearing his own thoughts finding expression
In that one central, swelling orison
Which now came sounding through the brooding
    night
With such distinctness, such impressiveness,
And searching cadence, that the very stars
Did seem to listen, as the voice concluded :

" But yet is hope within us ! for, our God,
Thy promise to the seed of Abraham,
And unto Israel in his closing hours,
And much that Thou hast done for this, thy people,
Bids us not yet to think that all is lost,
But fast and pray, and cry aloud for help
To Thee, Jehovah, whence aid only cometh
And timely succor. Help us now, O God,
And strengthen Thou the queen, even Queen Esther

The beautiful and good, in her great suit
And perilous plea for our deliverance
Before Ahasuerus, by whose law,
Procured by Haman for our overthrow,
We are condemned to slaughter. Thou, O God,
Knowest the hatred of our enemies,
And seest Thy people bowed with heavy grief,
And hearest their lamentations, and their prayers,
Pleading Thy mercy, and Thy intercession,
In this, the time of their most deadly peril.
And shall all Jewry be exterminate?
Shall Israel and Judah be cut off
So that the earth shall know no more of them?
And by a people who avow Thee not
Nor bend the knee unto Thee? Woe is me!
And woe to all Thy people everywhere
Unless Thou aid us! Lo, the days are sad,
Yea, and the nights are troubled with the cries
Of children, the low wailings of our women,
The shouts and moanings of distracted men
In garments rent, and strewn with dust and ashes
Mourning for Israel's doom. Turn it aside,
O God! Let us not perish in Thy sight
Like beasts brought to the slaughter! Save us,
    Lord!
Save or we die!"

Then as the prayer ceased
The multitude did lift their voices up
In a weird, suppliant chant, intoning all
The notes of grief and music of despair
In their impassioned words, while here and there
A tone of triumph, bursting from some soul
Fired with abiding faith in the Almighty,
Rang out above the rest, in strength and joyance
Temp'ring the doleful voices all around
With something of the leaven of bright hope,
While thus all chanted :

SONG OF THE MULTITUDE.

" God of our fathers, hear our pray'r !
O Abraham, thou intercede !
Isaac, let thy great spirit lead
Our thoughts to God in our despair !
Plead for us, Jacob ! fathers, plead !
God of the Hebrews, raise Thy hand
Or else we perish from the land !

" Jehovah, God, Oh, we have sinned,
And we have suffered much, and long,
And suffering now we pour our song
Of sorrow on the passing wind.

O God, protect us ! Thou art strong
And we are weak ! reach forth Thy hand
Or else we perish from the land.

" Thou sentest Joseph, bondman, led
Down into Egypt to be kept
Till Canaan's Land was famine-swept,
When Israel's remnant, following, fed
On surplus he had stored when reapt
As Thou hadst ordered. So Thy hand
Preserved them in the stranger's land.

" And when down-trod in servitude,
And writhing under Mizraim's heel
They felt the bitterness those feel
Who toil for bondmen's dole of food,
Then didst Thou answer their appeal ;
And Moses, as Thou raised'st Thy hand,
Did lead them from that heathen land.

" When Sennacherib's Assyrian host—
A countless horde in armèd might—
With threat'ning power invested quite
The walls 'round Zion, with proud boast
To level them, and put to flight
Thy people, lo ! Thy potent hand
Did smite the boasters in our land.

" O God, Thou knowest now the fate
Decreed against us ; the keen sword
Is whetted for our blood, O Lord ;
Our enemies are strong ; their hate
Is fierce and bitter as the word
Of foiled Abaddon ; raise Thy hand,
Lord, else we perish from the land."

The chanting ceased, and a low moaning plaint
Fervid, but indistinct, yet fraught with sorrow,
Came to their listening ears, and turning then
The woman spake unto the child and thus. :

" What meaneth this ?   Some mighty trouble hangs
Over this people surely, or their souls
Could not give voice to such weird song of woe,
And supplication for their God's protection
As we have listened to.   Go, little maid ;
Run but a moment to the aged Jewess
Who dwells near Gihon's pool, not far away,
And is bedridden, yet of ready speech—
She whom so often thou hast told me of
As being kind and confident to thee—
And learn, if learn thou canst, what has befallen
Her mourning people."

Then, without ado,
The child departed out into the night
On her strange errand, and the woman watched
And watching waited, waited till the day
Broke in upon the night, nor yet returned
The obedient little messenger she'd sent
To do her bidding ; and her heart was wrung
With apprehension, and her self-upbraidings
'Scaped from her pallid lips incessantly :

" Why did I send the child forth in the night
To learn of trouble that I might have guessed
From what I heard coming from out the darkness ?
And now 't is on the lips of passers-by
Wailing for Jewry.   My poor little Meta,
Without one word of plaint ; obedient
In all things, loving, true, and dutiful :
Never a word's dissent she uttered, though I now
Remember she looked pale as she went out.
Poor little heart ! perhaps 't was chilled with dread,
For surely the sad wailing of the people,
Coming from out the stillness of the night,
Were full of awfulness and weird concern,
And specially for one so very young.
Why did I bid her go ? for now I see
A thousand then-unthought-of dangers rise

To meet my darling.   Oh, my troubled heart !
I thought I had lost all 't could give thee pain—
That nothing in the world again could waken
Thy pulsings into throbs of agony,
But thy wild beating 'gainst my aching bosom
At this poor little waif's returning not
Oppresses me almost beyond endurance !
I must go out and seek her."

                                So she rose
And, drawing close a veil about her face,
Set out in search of the loved missing one,
And to the hovel near to Gihon's pool
First turned her steps, and as she went along,
On every hand she heard the voice of prayer,
The song of lamentation, and the speech
Of overhanging doom, and saw the signs
Of mourning and deep sorrow.   At her house
She found the Jewess, shrivelled with.old age,
And helpless with a cureless malady,
Stretched on her bed of years, and all alone,
(Her sole attendant having gone without)
Bemoaning weakly with unsteady voice—
Rising in invocation, falling in wails—
Prospective death to her and all her people,
And weeping bitterly as one in love

With life and joys which she was loth to leave,
But when she saw the woman at the door
She bade her enter.

To the simple query
If she had seen the child the night before
The Jewess said she had. " The child," she said,
Had "started quickly back unto her mistress
After inquiring of the Jewish sorrow,
Which it was strange that any should not know."
And then she straight detailed, without a halt,
The pending fate that threatened Israel
And how the queen had promised intervention
At her great peril. After hearing this,
The woman, bowing low, excused herself,
And, passing out, pursued her quest again
With heavy heart, the poor old Jewess' moans
Still sounding in her ears as she went on ;
But so it was whithersoe'er she went
Throughout the Jewish quarter. Mourning, tears,
And prayers, and lamentations, riven raiment,
And people prostrate wailing in the dust,
Were, round her everywhere, and, if she spake
To 'quire about the child, none noticed her,
For in the general sorrow few had thought
Save of calamity that threatened all.

And so she found no trace of whom she sought
All through that long and weary day of sorrow ;
Then, turning, heart-sick, sought her own poor hovel,
Half hoping that the lost one might be there,
Returned before her, but it was not so,
And she sat down and wept, in her poor shelter,
And weeping prayed, and praying spake aloud :

VASHTI'S PRAYER.

" O Sun, that deigns to shine on so much woe,
Lend not thy light unto it any more !
O, Aura-Mazda, in thy plenteous might
Turn yet aside the torrent of destruction
Which threatens to o'erwhelm this stranger people
Unwillingly among us ! Lo, it seemeth
As though the baleful strength of Ahriman
Would overcome all good. Stay him, All-Wise
And Bounteous One ! stay the power of Evil—
Fierce Angra Manyus, stalking now abroad
So full of cruel doing. Stay his hand,
And save this smitten people ! Many times
Of late I 've bowed unto thee, off'ring pray'r
For my unworthy self ; pleading my woes,
My disinheritance and fallen state,
As cause for intercession, to the end
That thou, at least, teach me obedience

And meek submission to thy holy will
(If so it be that I shall live and suffer)
And the King's pleasure. Still, although my griefs,
Lately so many, yet are multiplied,
My eyes but now are opened, and I see
That I have thought too much upon myself,
For, even now, what I alone do grieve
Is suffered many fold by many thousands
Unhappier than myself, and with more cause ;
For, it can not much matter that one soul
Is tortured in this world or taken from it,
But when a Race is threatened with extinction,
A homeless Nation, moaning as one man
And weeping as one woman, lying prone,
Calls out for mercy and commiseration,
It is a spectacle to move the gods,
And do thou heed it, great Ahura-Mazda !
In thy sweet mercy grant this Jewish queen—
This Esther whom, 't is said, is beautiful,
She who is raised whence I have been torn down—
To move the King's compassion, and forbid
That she too fall beneath his causeless wrath ;
And of my little maid, Oh, care for her !
That evil may not reach her where she is,
Or near, or far, from me who love her so.
Grant peace and quiet unto weary souls."

BOOK VI.

ESTHER.

L O, now the time was come to make her suit,
  And Esther, unattended and unbidden,
Clad in her royal robes and matchless beauty
Appeared before the King in his great hall
Seated in state on his imperial throne ;
And there she stood a time with downcast eyes
Challenging death, till the astonished King,
Struck with her beauty and her awful daring,
Stretched forth the golden sceptre in his hand
Giving her favor ; then bade her approach
Saying unto her :

          "Esther, my fair queen,
What is thy wish ? Fear not to make it known !
It shall be granted thee, even to the half
Of this great kingdom which I joy to share
With thee, Light of my Soul."

To which the queen :
" O King ! if I be favored in thy sight,
Come, even now, to-day, unto a banquet
Which I have spread for thee, and bring thou Haman
With thee."
So was it done, and as they drank
There of the ruddy banquet wine of Shiraz,
The King still prest her of her purpose, saying :
"What is thy petition ?" (Knowing well
The queen had not yet spoken her desire)
" But make it known, and lo, it shall be granted
Without condition, as I once have said."
And Esther answering :

"O most royal King,
If I have found thy favor, and it please
Thee still, O King, to grant me my request
And hearken my petition, let me pray
That thou and Haman come, yet once again,
Upon the morrow to another banquet
That I shall make for you ; then, please the King,
I may make known the thing that troubleth me,
Asking the King's indulgence, and his favor
For my petition."

Then went Haman forth
Joyful, and glad of heart at his preferment,

And as he passed the King's great palace front
Lo, there sat Mordecai in the gate
And stood not up to greet him, nor yet moved,
Nor deigned to notice the proud Agagite,
Who strode imperiously by, filled up
With angry indignation at the Jew.
Yet chid he not aloud the Jew's contempt
But through his teeth he muttered as he passed :

" Accursed Israelite ! I thought ere now
From what I've heard of thy most abject wailings
And loud implorings to thy unknown God,
That thy contemptuous spirit were subdued
And thy stiff neck were yielding to the yoke
That I have placed upon it, and thy peoples'
To drive and goad them on to death withal ;
And yet dost thou defy me, yea and worse,
Before my very eyes ; I will not bear it !
If I have power to compass the destruction
Of all thy cursed race at a fixed time,
What curbs my will to have thee taken off
A few days earlier than all the rest
With special ignominy, for thy pains
Of silent insolence ? and as example
To all thy fellows of a less degree,
And thus deprive thee of the hope of glory,

Which I believe that thou dost entertain,
Of being chief and leader of a host
The greatest that the world hath ever seen
Marching upon a given day to death
Without escapement. Yea, I 'll so devise."

So, walking on, the stony-hearted Haman
Warm with the wine he 'd drank, proud with success,
Angered at his ignoring by the Jew
And gloating o'er his prospect of revenge—
His soul a chaos of contending passions—
Came to his house and called his wife, and friends,
To whom in boastful strain he spake, recounting
The number of his sons, his growing greatness,
The measure of his riches, and the glory
And power wherewith the King had clothèd him ;
Of the great honor that the Queen had shown him
And of the morrow's pleasing invitation :
But while he talked the thought of Mordecai
Came on him and he spake again with rage :
" Yet all availeth nothing, while this Jew—
This hook-nosed Hebrew, sneereth his defiance,
From the King's gate, upon me, as he sitteth,
And stirs my soul to anger ! "
                                      Then his wife,
The sympathizing Zaresh, and his friends

Proposed the building of a lofty gallows
Whereon the offending Jew might speedily
Be hanged in sight of all the populace.
" And let the gallows be "—Zaresh advised—
" Made fifty cubits high, and on the morrow
Speak thou unto the King, that Mordecai
Be hanged thereon, then go, and merrily
Betake thee to the banquet." And the thing
Pleased Haman much, so that he straightway caused
The gallows to be made, nor could he rest
Until the morrow ere he sought the King,
But forthwith went unto the outer court
There to await until the King appeared
At early morn, that then he might request
The thing which so engrossed him.

                     Now it chanced
That when the King, returning from the banquet,
That night had stretched himself upon his couch,
His soul was troubled and he could not sleep,
But tossed upon his bed uneasily,
Gazing into the darkness with wide eyes,
While his deep heart-throbs shook his sturdy frame
And pulsed with feverish force in his hot temples
Rousing his mind to double wakefulness
In the oppressive silence, by himself,
And with his thoughts. Communing with himself,

At length, as though to break the stifling spell
That seemed to clasp him 'round with viewless arms,
He muttered to himself :
                    " And is this glory ?
Is this, then, greatness ?   True, I rule a world
Of goodly kingdoms and broad provinces
(The joint fruits of a wide inheritance
And of my own good sword and conq'ring hosts)
Whose people and whose princes, yea, and kings,
Do all proclaim me ' King ' with servile shouts,
And 'King of Kings ' with show of loyalty,
Yet how much boots it all ?   One heavy stroke
Of fell disaster,—one severe defeat
Of Persia's arms upon some foreign field—
One month's desertion by great Aura-Mazda
Would turn a hundred daggers at my throat
Aimed by the kinglets who despise my yoke
And claim to love me only that they fear
The scourge of my displeasure, and the rage
Of trampling armies thund'ring at their gates.
So only in my power is lodged my glory,
My greatness, in the strength of conq'ring hosts,
And, if the gods ordain, within one day,
I may be robbed of both.   And what of both ?
Upon the morrow would a million men
At my command take up the tools of war

To do my bidding, and a hundred kings
Send goodly store of tribute to the crown
From ev'ry part of this far-reaching empire ;
Yet here, at my own court, in mine own house,
I am at times a puppet, a bound slave
To the designing princes who are 'round me
And lash me into anger with their speech
And then frame words for me to voice my wrath
Unto their own advantage. Thus it is,
No man in all the kingdom, save the King,
But that might rule in his own family,
Within the law, according to his wish,
Without suggestion, hint, or interference :
But to the King, e'en this much is denied
By those who feign to serve him. Nor, forsooth,
May he e'en take unto himself a wife
But they must fix the manner of his wooing.
So, have I been harassed, and otherwise,
Here in my court at Shushan. While I am worn
With great perplexities and cares of state,
One asketh this, another prays for that,
Even of the few that I permit to come
Anear me, till I scarcely know the half
Of what is asked, or even what is granted
In my desire to be soon rid of them ;
Yet the King's word, when given, is as law.

And now of this petition of the queen,
Which is already granted ere the naming,
It yet concerneth me what she may ask,
For well her conduct doth to me portend
Some weighty matter that she hath in hand,
Else had she not, unbidden, sought my presence
Staking her life on meeting my approval ;
Faith, she is brave as well as beautiful
And I could not deny, ask what she might,—
Unless she come unto me speaking lies.

" Thus am I hedged about ! My boasted power
Filched from me by fair looks and honeyed words—
By promises and dark insinuations—
By cunning, and intrigue, and treachery,
And so, mayhap, is evil sometimes done,
And in my name, that should not know my name ;
While murd'rous treason, here within the palace
Would strike me lifeless from my jewelled throne
With less compunction than a shepherd boor
Might club a robber filching from his flock.
HO, GUARDS! THERE! LIGHT THE HALL, AND CALL
  THE SCRIBES !
AND BID THEM BRING THE BOOK OF CHRONICLES
AND READ TO ME THEREFROM THE LAST MONTH'S
  RECORD !"

The lamps, soon lighted, in the royal chamber,
Disclosed two golden guardsmen 'bove the door
Upon a mantel of veined Tabriz marble
Standing, half sidewise turned, in stern resolve
Crossing their jewelled spears before old Time—
A figure bald, and bearded, bent and grim—
Who, for a staff, leaned on the crystal tube
Of a gemmed clepsydra ; and so seemed Time
Himself denied admittance to the King ;
But the old tyrant's babes, the busy Hours,
Stole in atwixt the spears, and on the glass
The imprisoned water told the second watch,
Standing at level on the mark of midnight,
As the scribes entered ; when they sate and read
From out the chronicles, before the King
As they were bidden.   When at length they read
How Mordecai had disclosed the plot
Of the two chamberlains to slay the King,
The King inquired :
                              " What honor hath been done
To Mordecai ? and what dignity
Conferred upon him for this timely act
In our salvation ? "
                              Answered then the scribes :
" O King, there hath been nothing done for him
In honor, or reward, or circumstance,

Save the approval that a loyal soul
Must feel within itself for such a deed."
Then the King queried : "Who is in the court?"
And the King's servants answering said to him :
" Behold, even Haman standeth in the court
As if in waiting!" And the King exclaimed :
" Let him come in ! "
     And so came Haman in
And as he entered the King asked of him :
" What shall be done unto the man whom I,
The King, delight the most to honor ! "
       And now Haman
Within his heart bethought him thus:
       " To whom
Than to myself would the great King delight
To do more honor?" And still thinking so,
Answered the King :
     " Let thou the royal robes
Which on occasion the great King doth wear,
And so the horse which thus the King doth ride,
And the crown royal from the kingly head,—
Let all these things, and straightway, be delivered
Unto one of the King's most noble princes
That he may have the man arrayed, withal,
Whom the great King doth much delight to honor,
And bring him, mounted, through the streets of Shushan,

Proclaiming, too, before him, in the city
His well-earned glory.   Thus shall it be done
Unto the man whom the great King would honor."
When the King, answering Haman, spake, and thus :

" It is well said !   Make haste, take thou the apparel,
My crown, and royal steed, to Mordecai,
The Jew that sitteth oft in the King's gate
And do unto him as thou well hast spoken,
Failing in nothing."

Then went Haman out
In agony and deep humiliation
To do as bidden ; and throughout the city
(When the first sunny hours of day had come)
Preceding Mordecai—like the King
Arrayed and horsed—he called aloud :
" Thus shall it still be done unto the man
Whom the great King delighteth much to honor ! "
And when 't was over, with a heavy heart
Did Haman hasten mourning to his home,
With his head covered and his garments rent
Boding much evil ; and his wife and friends
Mourned with him, and his wise men prophesied
That now the Jew would e'en prevail against him,
And while they yet were talking there did come

The King's own chamberlains to bid him hasten
Unto Queen Esther's banquet.
                          So they came,
The King and Haman, straight unto the banquet
And as they sate again before the queen
This second day of banqueting and wine
The King inquired again :
                          " What is thy wish
Queen Esther? What is thy petition ? Speak !
Be not afraid, but make thy object known,
And it shall be performed, and granted thee
Unto the giving of one half my kingdom."
When, Esther, paling, answered thus :
                          " O King !
If I have found thy favor, let me first
Petition thee to give me my poor life,
And then request of thee to spare my people ;
For we are sold and given unto death
Without condition. If 't were only so
We had been sold to bondage, men and women,
And all our babes condemned to that estate,
I would have held my peace and bowed my head
Under the weight of a so deep affliction
Thinking it were God's will, to further punish
The sins of Israel ; for even so
Some little hope might live amongst our people—

Some gleam of dawn break through the awful darkness
For those that might come after us ; but death,
Coming at once, and unto our whole race—
The thought of it hath blanched our strongest men
And set all Israel mourning ; for the enemy
Exulteth at our fall, and only thou
May'st countervail our damage."
                              Then the King :
" Who is he, and where is he, that durst
Presume to do the things which thou hast said
To thee, or to thy people ? "
                              And the queen :
" The adversary and the enemy
Is now before thee ! 'T is this wicked Haman
Who would destroy us."
                              Then the King was wroth,
And rising from the banquet went without
Into the palace garden for a time,
And Haman pale with fear, plead for his life
Unto the queen, sinking upon his knees
Before her on the couch whereon she sate,
Begging for mercy ; when the King returned,
And seeing which he burned with jealous rage
And spake his fierce displeasure. Hearing this
The attendants seized the wretched Haman there,
Cov'ring his face and dragging him away,

While thus Harbona, the chief chamberlain
Delighting still to witness pain, and death,
And hating much the crafty Agagite
Spake calmly to the King :
     " Behold, O King ! ˙
Beyond the palace court, near Haman's house,
Yon towering gallows, fifty cubits high,
Which, only yesternight, did Haman build
For Mordecai, who hath saved the King
From the assassins' daggers."
       Angered still,
Gazing one moment on the giddy gibbet
With ready loop dependent from its arm,
The King spake briefly thus :
     " Hang him thereon ! "
So the poor wretch was dragged away to death.
But Esther pleaded still before the King
Casting herself in tears down at his feet,
Speaking her kinship unto Mordecai,
Thanking the King for what he 'd done for him,
And then continuing thus :
     " O King, forgive,
That I have brought this thing unto thy knowledge
Never till now ! But if this may not be,
And I have forfeited my claim to life,
I may have found some favor in thy sight

And though I die, O King, save thou my people !
Reverse the letters which the Agagite
Hath caused to be decreed condemning them !
For how can I endure that this great evil
Shall come upon them ?   How can I abide
The knowledge of their legalized destruction ?—
Their summary extinction from the earth ?
And so if my poor life might be their ransom
Unto thy own and God's transcendent glory
Glad would I yield it.   O my lord, my King !
Let me not plead in vain !——"

      So, passionate
And fervid in her tears and supplications,
Lain prone and pleading the tremendous cause
Of Israel condemned ; beseeching mercy
For all her race, e'en though herself might perish,
The deep strength of great sorrow in her voice,
Spake this fair woman, when the mighty King
Stretched o'er her prostrate form the golden sceptre,
Thus interrupting :

     " Lo, arise, Queen Esther ! "
And as she did so thus the King continued :
" Be calm and fear not ! for although the King,
Under our Mede-and-Persian precedents,
May not reverse that which is once decreed
More than our humblest subject, yet withal,

When gross duplicity and artful lies
Hath been employed to give an unjust measure
The seeming sanction of our royal name
With seal and signet and due attestation,
As in this matter there hath surely been,
Then may there be decreed some special edict
To break the force of the impending blow,
Or rob of power that which portends much evil ;
As in this case, the Jews might arm themselves
And stand for their own lives with our approval
Against all men soever who assail them,
And so avert destruction.   Mordecai,
Thy kinsman here, our own most trusty servant,
Is now empowered to draft, in our own name,
Even unto this purport, as he may
The needed letters royal."
                              As he spake
The King took from his hand his signet ring
And placed it on the finger of the Jew
While thus he added :
                              " Now our kingly power
And our imperial signet are with thee ;
Use them as seems thee best in this behalf,
And to our good queen's liking."
                              So it was :
The Jew, dictating to the royal scribes,

9

Caused letters to be writ and made of record
According to the power granted him
Signing the royal name, and, with a touch
He felt to be the ransom of his race,
Affixed the mystic signet to the scroll
Redeeming Israel ; for in Israel's sword,
With the law's sanction for its trusty wielding,
Was Israel safe. Then Mordecai came
Out from the presence of the mighty King,
Clad all in royal garb of blue and white,
With robe of Tyrean purple, and fine linen,
And a great crown of gold upon his head,
Blazing with gems—all gifts of the great King—
And as he passed along the streets of Shushan
The people greeted him with mighty shouts
And bowed before him as in reverence,
And all the city seemèd wild with joy,
But more than all, the Jews were filled with gladness,
And light was in their households once again,
And mourning ceased, and sorrow's voice was dumb,
And tears were dried, and tattered garments shed,
Glad-voiced hozannahs went up from their homes
And thankful pray'rs for their deliverance
Were offered to the God of Abraham.
Blessings were asked upon the beauteous queen,

And hope and joy and gladness sprang like flowers
Up in their hearts.
        So was their sorrow drowned,
And when the time was come to slay the Jews
According to decree procured by Haman,
The Jews fought bravely in their own defence
O'ercoming their assailants ; for the fear
Of Mordecai (now grown much in favor
With the great King) was heavy on all those
Who sought his people's hurt, and many turned
To aid whom lately they would have destroyed,
And so the Jews prevailed, and many fell
Among their enemies, and Haman's sons
Were first, among the many slain at Shushan
On that first day, and so upon the next—
For lo, the queen had gained a second day's
Employment for the sword of Israel
Within the city and the palace Shushan—
Fell many there who sought the hurt of Jewry,
But all throughout the provinces beside
None fell but on the day at first appointed
Unto the Jews' destruction ; but throughout
Did Israel prevail, and so was saved,
And so had rest from all her enemies ;
And Mordecai caused it to be writ

With the queen's sanction and the broad approval
Of all of Jewry ; that the next two days—
Fourteenth, and fifteenth, of the twelfth month, Adar,
On each recurring year as time shall pass
Be by decree forever set aside
Among the Jews, through all the generations
That Israel shall endure, as days of joy,
And gladness, and rejoicing, and good cheer,
Of giving portions unto one another,
Of gifts and charities unto the poor,
And that the time thereof be called " Purim,"
That is, from " Pur," the lot, which Haman cast
For Israel's destruction, the deliverance
From which let Israel commemorate
Till all the race is gathered in the tomb
To slumber with the fathers.
                                    So it was,
And so had Israel peace and quietude
Through all the years Ahasuerus reigned.

BOOK VII.

THE FLIGHT.

" HOW strangely goes the world ! A year agone
Death's shadow lowered dark o'er Israel,
And so all Jewry mourned exceedingly,
With such a depth of sorrow and alarm
As most did make me doubt *I* had known sorrow ;
Yet these were those whose strength of enmity
Rejoiced at Israel's sufferings and the fate
That seemed in store for her. But all was changed—
Changed almost in an hour. For, those three days
And their succeeding nights of piteous prayer
Seemed answered of Jehovah, their great God,
To whom they prayed for their deliverance ;
For so did this fair queen persuade the King,
Even at the peril of her own young life,
To let it be decreed that the condemned
Might with the sword defend them from their foes :
And then what joy, and gladness, and rejoicing

There was among them all who so had mourned ;
While the derided race sprang into favor
Even 'mong those who 'd sought to persecute them ;
(Pretended favor, mayhap, born of fear)
Yet as I learn were very many slain,
And not a few of these among the Jews,
But many more 'mong those who sought their hurt.

" Still did each lawfully destroy the other
According to the mandates and decrees
Of this great realm—each drew his sword or dagger
To slay the other in the Great King's name
As bidden by unalterable fiat.
So did the State contend against itself
Ranging its people one against another
And countenancing both sides equally,
Save that the last expression of the law,
As seeming to be backed by latest favor,
Robbed those committed to the earlier law
Of half their wonted courage, and instead,
Filled them with weakening doubt and apprehension,
And so impelled them to their own destruction.

" O, would that law were justice ! Would that Power
Might realize its fallibility
And so exert itself to do the right

According as it should be found in truth,
Instead of clinging to that stupid maxim
Which doth belie itself at every turn——
' *The King can do no wrong, he cannot err* ' ;
An idle claim to make for mortal man ;—
So this hath come to be this nation's boast :
' *Laws of the Medes and Persians never change.*'
O, shameful boast of a more shameful fact,
Which in this case filled four score thousand graves,
And crushed four times as many living hearts,
And all because a wicked man, and vain,
Had, by deception, in the Great King's name
Procured his wickedness to be made *law*—
Law, which, when shown in its enormity,
Might still not be expunged, nor yet repealed,
Because some unwise, thoughtless precedent
Hath been found in the ancient chronicles,—
And so, adhered to since without a question—
That what is written in the Great King's name,
And sealed with the King's ring, should be reversed
Never, by any power upon the earth.

" Thus folly, unrebuked, grows into custom,
And custom, written down, is precedent,
And precedent established, is as law,
And law may thus be builded on gross error

Which so secures its perpetuity,
Pledging the King and State, thus, in advance,
To its strict recognition and enforcement.
Surely things are awry in this strange world,
When kingly power may thus be pledged to wrong
Beyond revokement, and so, life or death
Be weighed upon a scale whose beam shall tip
As the mere shifting weight of accident
Shall be impelled along it.
     " Had the King
In this case—finding he had been deceived—
Annulled the product of the gross deception
And punished fittingly the base deceiver—
As erst he would but for the honored maxim
Whose close observance wrought this great dishonor—
And him alone, what bloodshed had been spared,
What innocent life redeemed from forfeiture !
So had wrong been rebuked and justice triumphed
In its own name, not trusting its enforcement
Into the hands of those whose bitter wrongs
Urged them beyond its bounds, and in its name
To strike fierce blows for vengeance.
     " This young queen
Whose beauty is the theme of ev'ry tongue,
Whose spirit and great courage are admired,
As I have chanced to hear, by all her people,

And by the populace of all the realm,
Was yet, from being bowed with a great sorrow—
Involving all her people, Israel,
Who tasted all the bitterness of death
And all the sense of a malign injustice—
Not raised thereby above that same injustice
From which her people suffered. But for this—
Though she is given all that I have lost,
And her great glory founded on the ruins
Of my own pulling down—I could have honored,
Yea, could have loved her with unstinted measure.

" Oh why should she, after that day's defence,
Which well insured her people's further safety,
Crave from the King another day of blood?—
A day of slaughter, and a day of vengeance,
Unclaimed of justice and bewailed of mercy ?
So fair in face and form, and so exalted
In her devotion to her harassed people,
I would for my own peace she had not stooped
To drink the bitter waters of revenge ;
The one thing only that doth seem to taint
The grand perfection of her womanhood.

" But why should I reflect on any soul
E'en though it only be unto myself,

Knowing, that I, myself am so imperfect?
Beside, I am condemning her unheard,
The very thing myself did most complain of.
Yet, after all, what matters my poor words
Of condemnation, favor, or applause?—
The idle comments of a friendless creature,
Who,—like a child that talks to lifeless toys,
Then lends its voice to frame their answers in,—
Finds pastime listening to her own speech.

" O, how I long to see my little Meta!
Poor child, I did delight to talk with her,
And teach her, as I might, some little good;
Her company was as one cooling spring
In the parched desert of my loneliness.
'T was only yesternight I dreamed of her
The sweetest dream, fruit of my squalid bed,
That not a vision of my best estate
On cushioned couch of ivory and gold
E'er equalled.　I was a child, I dreamed,
Playing beside a shallow, pebbly lake
Fed from the waters of the Pactolus
By spraying fountains ranged about the shores;
And milk-white swans were sailing near the centre
Which was as smooth and placid as a mirror;
And as I played there 'neath the full-leafed trees

That fringed the lake about and cast their shade
Upon the grassy sod abloom with flowers,
Lo, little Meta—as it seemed—for playmate
Was with me, and we laughed, and sang together,
And rollicked with a pretty, dappled fawn,
Which ran and skipped with us in playfulness,
Until, half wearied into restful mood,
We sate upon a sweet moss-covered bank
And gazed out on the lake where the swans lay
Riding the glassy surface in their beauty
And moving grace, till, as the day advanced,
And the bright sun grew warmer in the sky,
These, like white, fairy ships came sailing in
As from far voyage, and when near the shore
They dallied 'neath the playing fountain jets
Pluming their snowy down in sportive mood,
Beating the falling spray with lifted wings
And revelling in joyous, sportive humor
Which seemed a part of all things.
                              " In a cove—
A mossy indentation in the shore—
A tiny shallop floated daintily,
Not tightening the white-linked shining chain
That held it to its moorings ; and in this
We lightly stepped, loosening its silver bonds,
And paddled out a distance on the lake

Till on our view, above the sloping wood,
The domes and turrets of a mighty city
Rose clear against the background of Mount Tmolus
Silent, serene, majestic. This was Sardis !
One time so glorious and magnificent—
The builded dream of Crœsus wrought in stone,
And brass, and gold, the marvel of the world—
And still a city full of wealth and splendor ;
And this was Lydia, my native land !
And this, my happy dream the duplicate
Of many, many of my childhood's days."

As thus soliloquized the outcast queen
A muffled figure clad in woman's garb,
Bent as from weight of years, and heavily
Leaning on a stout staff, and carrying
A grimy sack, which well proclaimed the beggar,
Pushed back the hut's rude door, and standing there
Spake in low tones unto the startled Vashti :

" Hush, woman ! Peace ! I am thy more than friend,
And come to offer thee deliverance
As one attached to thee by ties of blood,
And bound to thee by sense of loyal duty ;
And therefore, listen ! " (Having shut the door
The strange intruder faced the half-dazed woman

And thus continued :) " As a little child
I saw thee oft about thy home near Sardis
Where also I did dwell, and knew thy father,
Who was my father's brother, kinsmen both
Of mighty Crœsus, who died here in Persia
A royal prisoner of the great Cyrus—
Nay interrupt me not, but be thou free
From fear of treachery or thought of evil
And hear me further :
          " Now a year agone,
A nomad band of Bactrians from the East
Came wandering through the Lydian settlements
Bartering rich Indian stuffs for Lydian gold
And entertaining idle curious crowds
With magic conjurings and wondrous feats
Of hand-sleight and mysterious necromancy.
Among the rest, a little Persian maid
Was of the band—slave of the company—
Whom when they came to Sardis, there, they sold
In the slave market of the famous city :
My aged sire from sympathetic venture—
Feeling a curious interest in the child
Not knowing why 't was so—bid in the waif ;
And this same little slave hath many times,
Since coming to our house, told of a night—
A night of gloom and wailing here in Shushan—

A night of awful mystery, when she went
Out on an errand for a much-loved Mistress,
Whom she hath oft described, and wept about,
Saying : ' They took me from her in the darkness—
My cries unnoticed in the general wailing—
And carried me away unto the camp
Of those ye bought me of—a kidnapped slave,
And now a slave by purchase—— ' "
                                        Here a groan
'Scaped from the woman seated in the hut,
Who thus half sobbing spake :
                                        " Poor little soul !
How hath she suffered—suffered for my sake
Who am not worthy.   My own suffering
Is chiefly, now, the suffering that comes
From knowledge of the suffering of others
Borne for my fault—albeit unwitting fault—
Or for the show of sympathy with me :
But whom art thou who speakest many truths
And seemest so possessed of certain knowledge,
And yet in thine own person doth belie
The very truths thou seekest to proclaim ?—
Truth heralded by falsehood !   Yet this fact
Hath like its purpose, so I ask thee further—
Whom, thinkest thou, am I ?   save as thou seest
A poor and unknown woman, lone and wretched ? "

To which, the stranger thus : " First, to thy last :
This which thou sayest, in a certain sense,
Might fix thy state and evident condition,
But, as thou 'st intimated of myself,
The truth is not consistent with thy seeming,
But truth is aye consistent with itself,
And, be the *whole* truth known there is no puzzle
In that which but a *part* involves us in ;
So words of truth from a poor little slave,
Fitted to other truths, which I have learned.
All, now sustained by what I see and hear,
Proclaim thee as the child I knew at Sardis,
Joy of a Lydian house, light of a home,
One time the pride of Persia, and her queen,
Dishonored without fault, blamed for no wrong,
Banned at the instance of designing men—
A princess, queen, a martyr to injustice——"

" Hush, whomsoe'er thou art ! " the listener cried,
" Know that thy words are treason to the King !
And that thy life, should these words go abroad,
Must surely pay the forfeit——!"
                              " Loyal soul !
I know the danger that thou speakest of,
But only thou dost hear, and so I fear not,
For thou art loyal and yet merciful

As have been all the members of thy house ;
And now I may proceed to answer further
Thy double query.   Well enough thou knowest
Thou hadst no cousin in thy early home,
Of thy own sex, as also I well know,
Hence seems the contradiction of my story
In my own person which thou spakest of,
For thou rememberest little Aldiphernes,
Rough playmate that he was, and mayhap prone
At times to little acts of selfishness,
And boisterous withal ; and he still lives,
And he hath heard from this same little slave,
The story that hath brought me to this place,
Sought out by his untiring love and zeal,
To do thee helpful service.   Raised a soldier,
He hath assumed the calling of a merchant,
Coming ostensibly from Cappadocia,
With wares and peltries from Mount Amanos,
To trade in Shushan.   Now, his merchandise
He hath disposed of, and his caravan
Being reladen for his quick return,
He fain would have thee go with him at once
Back to thy own loved Lydia, where a home
Peaceful and quiet hath been made for thee
Beyond intrusion and discovery—
Beyond the malice of the wrathful King

Which even now sleeps in forgetfulness,
Or is o'ershadowed by the dire disaster
To Persia's arms at far Thermopylæ,
And her magnificent fleet 'whelmed in destruction
In the consuming fight on Salamis,
At which the Great King still is exercised
And troubles much, as I have lately heard,
Now mourning for the loss of his great host,
Now vowing furious vengeance on the Greeks,
And now plunged deep in black despondency,
Fearing the safety of his own great empire ;
So this distraction with affairs of State
Now maketh fleeing easy."

　　　　　　" What thou sayest"—
The astonished listener here interrupted—
" Fills me with nameless terrors and alarms ;
For though thou hast informed me whom I am
And kindled in my heart a ray of hope—
Hope that but brings to life new power to suffer—
Thou hast not yet proclaimed to me thyself
Nor intimated to me in what manner
I should elude the eyes of those who know me,
If not for what I was, for what I am.
Should I be seen set out and not return
Then might some inquiry attract attention,
And this again, lead on to some disclosure

10

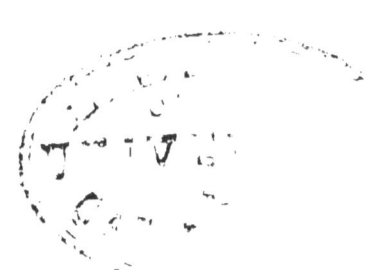

To spur pursuit, and then, if overtaken,
Think of the brave man whom thou sayest sent thee,
And what were then his fate.   Beside, what right
Have I, but to abide the punishment
Which is decreed against me ? and this step
Might bring swift harm to many innocent souls,
Then wherefore should I take it ? "
                                        Unto which
The unknown gave this further in reply :

" Nay, then believe not thus !   Dismiss thy fears
Of future ill to others, and attend,
For once, to thine own good ; for life is dear
When it may be with pleasure to ourselves,
Or profit unto others, lived withal ;
And, being innocent, there is no justice
Or claim of conscience to be satisfied,
Then to what end shouldst thou abide here longer,
In misery and want, by death ignored,
Yet living to no purpose but to suffer ?

" Now as to whom I am :   Deceit is folly,
And acting that which is not verity
Is lying, with the lack of hardihood
To falsify by simple word of mouth ;
Yet would I not be deemed a fool or liar,

For though I am not what to thee I seem
Still am I that I now *would* seem to thee,
And yet forestall surprise, belay alarm,
And to the world without, which may have eyes
Even for the darkness, give no single hint
That I am other than I seem to be :
This much our safety and the time demands,
And this confessed I now may crave thy pardon
And say that 'neath this beggar's cowl and cloak,
Looking upon thee from behind this veil,
Thy kinsman Aldiphernes stands, thy servant,
Faithful to death for thy deliverance.

" Nay, mention not thy scruples, or my danger,
Nor waste thy time in speaking gratitude.
The first I hope may quickly disappear,
The second I opine is really naught,
The last I well believe ; though I 'm unworthy,
For well I know, I can but do my duty
If I succeed in doing all I wish
For one so worthy and withal so noble :
I only grieve the hard necessity
Which hath compelled this awkward subterfuge
To aid my search, and now for further plans :
My wife hath made this pleasant journey with me,
She hath a maid who will not yet return
.

And thou shalt dress as she doth and be maid
In seeming to Aryenis my wife.
So shall we go our way without suspicion ;
Come then, at midnight unto Zora's pool,
Where is our caravan encamped even now ;
Array thyself in this light Lydian tunic."
(Saying which, a parcel from the ready sack
He handed to the woman.) "Now will I
Proceed before thee, and in proper dress
Conduct thee to the tent of Aryenis
When thou hast reached our camp, and on the mor-
    row
Shall we set out for Lydia and new life."

So was it, and next day the camp was broken,
And they set out upon the travelled way
Up the Chaospes on its western bank ;
Vashti beside her kinsman's wife, both mounted
On Cappadocian steeds, lively, yet gentle ;
And Aldiphernes joined them oftentimes
As day by day they journeyed leisurely,
Now close behind the moving caravan
And now again a little distance back,
Passing the time in pleasant social converse.

'T was as another life and dream to Vashti ;
Freedom, fresh air, bright birds, and blooming flowers

Were all about her pouring out their sweets—
Intoxicating every sense with pleasure.
An unwalled landscape, and an unvexed sky
Dispelled all but the memory of restraint
From her long-fettered spirit, setting hope
And thankfulness aglow within her heart ;
And each new day discovered some new joy
Or brought to sense some cause of gratitude
For this long-suffering woman.
                                    As they passed,
One lovely evening of a perfect day,
Along the margin of a narrow valley,
They heard a cowherd singing 'mong his kine
Close by the foothills spurring out from Zagros,
Words that inspired her as the herdsman sang :

SONG OF THE COWHERD.

" I have no thirst for spoils or war,
I care no single jot for fame,
But e'er the breezy pastures far
Unvexed by care, and free from blame.
I tend at will the sweet-breathed kine !
Once Yima's charge, now, haply mine.

" With these I tarry day by day,
And night by night they hedge me round,

For I 'm their king ; my subjects they,
Prompt and obedient at the sound
Of voice or horn ; my gentle kine,
Great Mithra's charge as well as mine.

" And so, in all their hours and moods
We see the days and know them well ;
From midnight's star-lit solitudes
To sunny noontide's golden spell
We know the hours, I and my kine,
Great Mithra's charge as well as mine.

" When bends the grass with jewelled drops,
And Mithra from the Holy East
Lays hands upon the mountain tops
And steps into the world, I feast
On Morning's pomp, these eyes of mine,
While feast on dewy blades the kine.

" From midday's hot and searching sun
'Neath shade of plane trees and chinars
We seek our rest ; and one by one
With sighs of ease, which nothing mars
They lie contented down, my kine,
While sleep, all undisturbed, is mine.

" At night the sacred fire aglow
Guards us, from Zagros' altars high,

While blazing constellations show
The far sweet pastures of the sky
Where may I sometime roam, my kine,
Then, Mazda's charge as well as mine.

" Thus 't is, I would not change my state
To be earth's mightiest of men,
For Mithra looks compassionate
Upon the kine ; so, fitly, when
I and my herd shall pass, 't were mine
'Yond Chinvat Bridge ¹ to tend the kine."

So the song ceased :
                    " A pretty chant indeed."
Thus, simply, spake Aryenis to Vashti.

" Yea, true, my gracious cousin, and a grand ; "
Replied the other, and then thus continued :
" Such rare contentment, such unbounded faith
In what one has, and what one hopes to have,
I ne'er before have heard find utterance.
If this poor herdsman truly hath the spirit
Which he hath voiced in what we 've listened to,
Then surely is he greater than a king
And happier than the happiest I have seen—
More to be envied than if store of gold

¹ The " Bridge of the Gatherer " across which souls must pass
into Paradise.

And power unbounded were at his command ;
For, having these, what mortal yet hath been
Content therewith, or happy in his state ?
But this poor swain exalts his humble station
Singing its favor with the immortal gods,
Hoping continuance here, and so, hereafter,
With only transfer to the heavenly pastures,
But asking, wishing, praying nothing better,
The while insisting that he hath the best.
Sure 't is a happy soul !　It hath been said
' The needs of men are few, their wants are many.'
But this one's wants hath not outrun his needs,
And if he sing the truth both are supplied.
It is a blessed soul."
　　　　　　　　Here Aldiphernes
Fell back and joined them for a time to say
The camp would be pitched for the night near by,
Where a sweet spring leaped from a giant rock
And ran across a level grassy space—
A lovely pasture for their hungry beasts.

BEFORE THE ROCK BEHISTUN.

Next day the travellers struck the ancient road
Leading from Babylon to Ecbatana,
And followed its worn course, veering to right,
Until they came to that great flowing pool,

And that fair vale, and that majestic script,
Associated long with war and song,
Loved of all Iran, sacred unto Ormazd,
And for a while they sate their patient beasts—
And gazed upon this scarped and polished page
Of great Behistun Rock, whereon was writ
In markings cuneiform and sculptured story
The history of Iran and the world—
The tale of Semiramis and her wars,
Her victories and conquests ; Cyaxeres',
The Mede's, great triumph o'er Assyria,
And Cyrus' mightier doings in the west—
The humbling of Crœsus, King of Lydia,
Led captive from sacked Sardis, crushed in spirit,
(His empire blotted, like a smitten bubble ;)
Belshazzar's slaughter, and great Babylon's fall ;
The captive Jews departing by decree
(Bearing the golden vessels in their hands)
To build once more the Temple of Jehovah ;
The coronation, next, of mad Cambyses,
Who next beneath the shadow of the Sphinx,
With his shod heel upon the Pharaoh's neck
Plunges his sword in Egypt's living faith,
The incarnated Apis.   Great Darius
Slaying with his own hand the pseudo Smerdis,
And with relentless force and energy

Crushing at once the Magian revolt,
And sending traitors forth to crucifixion ;
The questioning of a band of Scythian captives
About their far-off land beyond the Euxine ;
The story of his conquests far and near
And their most glorious issue, well portrayed
In one grand rugged climax wrought in stone—
The subject nations in Atlantean figures
Upholding in their might the conqueror
Seated in state upon a carven throne
Dictating to the world.
     Such was the tale
The beholders saw, and read, read there in silence,
Each one intent upon the mighty work
That Pride had planned and Wealth and Power brought
  forth
With years of toil, upon the upright face
Of the prodigious rock, and looking so
Each one no doubt in his or her own mind
Forming a different est'mate of the whole
When Vashti spake, and thus :
       " It seemeth strange
That this great towering rock, silent as death,
Old as the world is old ; and no doubt witness
To some o' the earliest of our boastful race

Passing its walls in their unguided quest
Of homes and food, all free and unopposed,—
Save as the elements, alone, opposed,—
And only troubled that the choice of lands
For very plenty made it hard to choose—
The good being left in weary search of better—
Hath come at last to tell of men's fierce struggles
In the depriving of their fellow-men
Of the possession of the land they chose,
By force and conquest !   Yet 't is surely so !
And only is the victor glorified,
E'en here as elsewhere, while the vanquishéd
With loss of country, loss of place and power,
Must here behold the keenest loss of all—
Loss of that spirit in the conqueror
To do a gallant foe no useless wrong,
Portraying on the everlasting rocks
His ruined state and deep humiliation.
Yet 't is a wondrous sight, and now do I
Well understand our Persia's pride in it ;
But let us on at once ; my life hath been
Such that this story now doth sicken me !
Still would I not have missed it for the world ;
'T will be a medicine for the hereafter,
So let us on, dear cousins, once again."

Then on again to northward, passing west
Of old Mount Elwend, to the eastern base
Of Zagros' towering range, where grassy vales
Pierce like green bays the rugged mountain headlands
And laughing streams dance down through lovely pas·
    tures
Where sheep and cattle graze and drink their fill,
And songs of shepherds echo 'mong the hills
That guard the valleys' flanks, and clustering groves
Cast grateful shadows through the heats of day
And shelter 'mong their boughs Night's minstrelsy
Locked in the bosom of sweet Philomel :
Thence on, and on, through ever-changing scenes,
Passing at length Lake Urumieh's shore
And thence away again trending to westward
Toward Lake Van of the enchanting islands :
Then turning northward still, trav'ling a time
Amid the famous pastures of the Araxes,
Then passing that famed stream, turned to the left
And gained the wooded flank and southern base
Of Ararat, on whose bare rocky cone,
Now like a vasty dome among the clouds,
Rested the Ark of Noah, that first ship
Whose sides of rugged plank well interposed
Betwixt the remnant of our sinful race
And sure destruction in a drowning world :

Then on again through fair Armenia
Into the ancient road from Nineveh—
The trail of armies and the path of war
In centuries past—and followed northward thence
Through eastern Cappadocia, over ground
Each rood of which was like a funeral slab
That breathed the living tale of the dead past.
" Here,"—Aldiphernes said unto the women
As they were riding through a lovely valley,—
" Breaking the barrier of the Caucasus
And following down the curving coast of Euxine
A space, then turning to the left and striking inland,
The fierce Cimmerians in our Gyges' reign,
First settled like a horrid human swarm
To spread themselves o'er all our Asia Minor,
The harbingers of bloodshed and destruction.
Rapine and slaughter followed in their course,
Gyges, the King, was slain in stubborn battle,
And Sardis was the first time razed with fire,
Her treasure seized by the barbarians,
Her soldiers done to death, her people butchered,
Save at the citadel which stood all onslaught ;
When the fierce bands retired to burn and pillage
In other towns.   Three generations passed !
Fierce war continuous and wasting death
Had weakened the hard foe, when Allyattes,

Great-grandson of King Gyges whom they slew,
With his victorious armies mad for vengeance,
O'er this same valley drave the fleeing remnant
Of the vast robber hordes limping from wounds
And lean with hunger to their frozen North."

" 'T is the same story ever, cousin ; " Vashti said,
" Man's fierce injustice, and God's retribution—
The endless struggle still forever raging
'Twixt Ahriman and great Ahura Mazda,
'Twixt Good and Evil.   But, go on, I pray thee !
I would not interrupt, but was intent
Upon thy words and spake before I thought."

" Here too, Cyaxeres, the conquering Mede
Assyria's fate, and doom of Nineveh,
Fresh from the overthrow of Saracus [1]—
Who made great Nineveh a funeral pyre
For his own body and his fallen empire—
Passed, conquering the Cappadocian State,
To cross the Halys and to there cross swords

[1] Ashur-emid-elin, the last of the Assyrian kings, called by the Greeks, " Saracus."

" Saracus, unable to resist them, took counsel of his despair, and after all means of resistance were exhausted, burned himself in his palace."

                                Rawlinson's *An. Mon.*, vol. i., p. 500.

With his great rival, Lydia's famous king—
The conqueror of the Cimmerians—
In unavailing war. First victory
Dwelt for a time with one, then with the other
Yet neither gained a permanent advantage
Till in a battle on the Phrygian plains
While the contending armies strove in fury,
And flights of arrows filled thc wounded air,
And clash of sword on sword and helm and shield,
And clang of spears and hurtling javelins
And crashing blows of battle-axe and mace,
And shouts of men in hate's intensity,
Groans of the wounded, sinking to the earth,
And the wild plunging of death-stricken steeds
Bearing down victims in their agony,
Made the day hideous with the din of war,
And flecked the trampled field with gouts of gore
And streams of trickling blood, until it seemed
That death would claim each soldier ere it ceased
So stubborn was the fray and so relentless ;
When the offended gods themselves, appalled
At the great carnage and terrific strife,
Smote light out of the sun, and hung with shade
The fleckless blue of the o'erarching sky [1]

[1] This engagement is known among Orientalists as the "Battle of the Eclipse."

So, sudden darkness fell upon the hosts
And dread seized on their hearts, and hate died out,
And the strife ceased in fear and awe and tremblings ;
A parley, then a lasting truce, ensued
Between the leaders of the opposing hosts,
And an alliance followed shortly after
'Twixt Allyattes and Cyaxeres,
The first giving his only daughter, named,
As our wife here is namèd ' Aryenis,'
In wedlock soon to the great Median's son,
Young Astyages.   So came peace and power
For many years to all of this fair region."

" A blessed ending," said the banished queen,
" To the long, cruel tragedy of war
And its last dreadful scene.   'T was Mithra's self,
I doubt not, growing sick at sight of blood,
Put up his hands before his shining face,
To shut from view the carnage and the slaughter,
Who thus brought darkness on the shuddering world
And stayed mid air the uplifted hand of Death :
Blest be his name therefor, forevermore."

So sped these later days ; the soldier, now
Within a region whose eventful past
From bardic song and patriarchal tale

Was like a well-known friend, thus-while declaring
Its legend and its history of old,
And the fair exile breathing quiet comment,
And judging all things by sweet Mercy's test,
And all in turn selecting from the present
Small themes for passing speech and pleasantry.

Now struck they first the Persian conquerors path,
And pressing onward still, they passed into
The famous district of Pteria,
Where, reaching a small plain, the soldier joined
Again his fair companions and spake thus :
" Here, the great Cyrus on his westward course,
With his vast armèd host, Persians and Medes,
First saw our kinsman the heroic Crœsus
Who 'd come to meet him in the shock of arms,
With his embattled Paphlagonians
And Lydians, and stout Ionian Greeks,
Mycians, Celicians, and proud Carians,
Phrygians, and men of Miletus and Dorians—
All gallant troops of Crœsus' own fair empire ;
And here was cast the first day's gage of battle—
And all day long the fight incessant raged
A chaos of contention, horsemen and foot
Raining fierce blows continuous ; forward and back
Swayed by the weight of onset, or recovering

With desperate courage and fierce energy
Regaining inch by inch the coigne of vantage,
Lost at the outset, to the waver line
Where each side fought as moveless as the hills,
Falling beneath each other's blows and thrusts
But yielding not ; stubborn to stand and fight
Yet wearied beyond effort of fresh onset;
Till in the dusk of eve, bleeding and shattered,
Each side withdrew from the betrampled field,
Strown with the dead, unblest of victory.

" Ere morn our Crœsus, counting o'er the cost,
And being less in number of his troops
Than Cyrus was, deemed it the wisest thing
At once to cross the Halys and retire
To his own capitol, the splendid Sardis,
Arriving whence, he then dismissed his troops
(Save his own Lydians) and telling them
To come again with the returning spring,
He deeming not the baffled bleeding foe
Would for a moment think to follow him ;
But lo ! before his allies had been gone
The full hours of a wedded day and night
Behold a trooper dashing through the streets—
His helmet and his armor and his shield
Cast from him to relieve his foaming steed—

Cried out. '*To arms!* THEY COME ! THE PER-
SIANS !'

" No time now to recall th' disbanded troops,
But ho ! the Lydian horse ! rider and steed,
Magnificent in courage, and well skilled
In all the movements of defensive war—
The Lydian horse were there, eager and brave ;
Fleet as the tempests breath and frosty keen
They fell upon the foe doubling his front
Back in confusion, then away again
Striking the bold invaders such fierce blows
In their terrific onset as now threw
The whole invading host into one whirl
Of broken ranks, and troops disorganized
In madding tumult. So did this brave band
Of matchless Lydian horsemen with swift blows
Bring dire confusion, promising defeat ·
To that whole host of Persians and stout Medes.

" Oh, deathless, deathless is their splendid valor !
O Lydia ! beloved of my soul !
Such was the swan-song of thy chivalry !
For on that fateful field, the last of all
On which thy sons might shed their blood for thee
Still beautiful, untrammelled, and unchained,

They well outdid their former mightiest deeds
And on the inconstant air, with their keen blades
Dipt in the rising sun, painted thy name
In rainbow hues across the wintry sky,
One glorious moment to be seen of men
And then fade out forever !
     " Prowess now
Must fail before a worse than juggler's trick
And courage, handicapped, yield no return,
For soon the wily Cyrus to the front
Urges a mounted band of dusky men
Riding on tawny camels, tall and gaunt,
Ungainly beasts, of unaccustomed form
And scent [1] to the astonished Lydian steeds
Which soon were wild with terror at the sight
And uncontrollable by their brave riders,
Who then dismounted, and so fought on foot,
And fell so fighting 'gainst o'erwhelming odds,
Continuing the struggle till the night,
When in the darkness, the remaining few
Withdrew into the strong-walled citadel
Where yet for weeks the people still held out ;
But Sardis fell at last, and Lydia died,

[1] Horse nature has not changed since those remote times, as the scent or sight of camels will fill the average horse of to-day, not used to them, with uncontrollable dread.—J.B.K.

All but in story, and her puissant king
Went forth a captive, never to return."

Now as they neared to Sardis, Aldiphernes
Stayed more among his drivers in the van ;
They reached the city early one fair night
And when the once queen and the little slave
Beheld each other, being left alone
They wrapt each other in a glad embrace
And told their troubles, since their parting, o'er,
And so renewed their love, that purest love,
The love of women of unequal birth
Unequal age, unequal gifts and knowledge,
The growth of equal suffering shared together,
And equal to all trials, to the end.

In a secluded vale near Hermes stream,
Within an ancient Lydian demesne
Whose splendid home had fallen sometime vacant—
When he who owned it fell in distant Greece,
A victim to great Xerxes' war for conquest—
The lights shone out again ; the fountain tubes,
Dry from disuse, again laughed joyously
Spurting with brazen lips their cooling showers ;
The long-neglected gardens bloomed anew,

And lovely walks, and bowers of quiet beauty,
Took form among the tangled greenery,
And tiny lakes smiled in bright emerald shores
To gem the sweet retreat where peace should come
To dwell with Vashti the long-outlawed queen,
Who here so found a fitting house of refuge
And lived in meditation, a recluse
With but her little friend the Persian maid,
And a few trusty servants. Here were passed
The best-contented and the happiest days
Of one so deeply wronged—THE NOBLEST WOMAN,
THE KINDEST SOUL IN A WHOLE MIGHTY EMPIRE,—
THE LOVELIEST HEATHEN THAT THE WORLD HATH
    KNOWN.